HOW TO BUILD
STAFF INVOLVEMENT IN
SCHOOL MANAGEMENT

Also by the Author

Complete Book of School Public Relations

HOW TO BUILD STAFF INVOLVEMENT IN SCHOOL MANAGEMENT

Donovan R. Walling

PRENTICE-HALL, INC.
Englewood Cliffs, NewJersey

Prentice-Hall International, Inc., *London*
Prentice-Hall of Australia, Pty. Ltd., *Sydney*
Prentice-Hall Canada Inc., *Toronto*
Prentice-Hall of India Private Ltd., *New Delhi*
Prentice-Hall of Japan, Inc., *Tokyo*
Prentice-Hall of Southeast Asia Pte. Ltd., *Singapore*
Whitehall Books, Ltd., *Wellington, New Zealand*
Editora Prentice-Hall do Brasil, Ltda., *Rio de Janeiro*

© 1984 by

PRENTICE-HALL, INC.
Englewood Cliffs, NJ

Second Printing.....July 1987

Library of Congress Cataloging in Publication Data

Walling, Donovan R.
  How to build staff involvement in school management.

  Bibliography: p.
  Includes index.
1. Teacher participation in administration.   2. Management committees.   I.   Title.
LB2806.W27   1984   371.1'06   84-4839

ISBN 0-13-403080-X

PRINTED IN THE UNITED STATES OF AMERICA

To Jim Burns

About the Author

Donovan R. Walling has experience as a teacher, administrator, department chairman, and union president, and has written numerous articles for professional publications, including *Educational Leadership, The Clearing House, English Journal*, and *Dramatics*. He has helped to design and implement gifted education programs in Sheboygan, Wisconsin, where he directed an ESEA Title IV-C project for the affective education of gifted students, and in Zweibruecken, West Germany, where he coordinated program planning and initiation of gifted education for the Department of Defense Dependent High School. Mr. Walling's work with gifted education is described in recent articles in the gifted education journal, *G/C/T* and *Roeper Review*.

As in his first book, *Complete Book of School Public Relations: An Administrator's Manual and Guide* (Prentice-Hall, Inc., 1982), Mr. Walling has focused on communications and human relations, bringing to bear his wide experience with staff-management interaction. His other published works include newspaper features, several poems in journals and anthologies, and a radio play for Wisconsin Public Radio. He has spoken on the topics of communication and creativity before both general and professional audiences in the United States, Canada, and West Germany.

Mr. Walling holds a bachelor's degree in art and English from the Kansas State Teachers College (Emporia State University) and a master's in curriculum and instruction from the University of Wisconsin–Milwaukee.

Why Involve Your Staff?

If you're tired of books about school management that concentrate on the theoretical and philosophical aspects of school administration, then this practical book is for you. *How to Build Staff Involvement in School Management* grows out of the conviction that effective administration depends on the meaningful involvement of staff members in the day-to-day and long-range management of schools.

Is this a book about school management by committee? The answer is, emphatically, *no*! The issue of participatory management is essentially one of authority. Using staff involvement techniques will not diminish the decision-making authority of school leaders—superintendents, principals, curriculum directors, specialists, or department heads—in fact, their authority is often enhanced.

Staff involvement in school management enriches educational programs by broadening levels of understanding, strengthens educational philosophy through shared concerns, heightens teacher job satisfaction through participation in matters vital to the total educational process, and expands the professionalism of all educators by promoting a common sense of purpose.

Most administrators at all levels of the educational management hierarchy would agree that these are powerful reasons for developing more effective approaches to staff involvement. Teachers want to be involved in the school management process because it directly affects them. Administrators want and need the support, leadership, and assistance that involved teachers can bring to the management function.

In a study reported in *Phi Delta Kappan*, the education fraternity journal, Robert J. Krajewski asked principals to rank order both the *realistic* and *idealistic* levels of their major responsibilities as administrators.* In the *realistic* ranking, principals rated being an administrator

---

*Robert J. Krajewski, "Secondary Principals Want To Be Instructional Leaders," *Phi Delta Kappan*, September 1978, p. 65.

—i.e., a manager—of school materials and facilities as their most prominent duty. However, in the *idealistic* ranking, principals rated being instructional and curricular leaders first in importance.

Clearly, most administrators desire those roles that cannot be achieved without strong support and involvement of their staffs.

Gail Linnea Thierbach at the University of Wisconsin produced similar evidence of a desire for involvement on the part of teachers.[*] Her study showed that staff involvement in the management process, particularly in the determination of the school's organizational structure, positively enhanced teachers' feelings of job satisfaction.

These studies and others make it clear that both teachers and administrators want to develop ways in which staff can be involved in the management of schools. But there are some stumbling blocks that must be considered, one significant consideration being the relationship between the school administration and the teacher union.

HOW MANAGEMENT AND UNION CAN WORK TOGETHER

Whenever notions arise about staff involvement in traditionally management-centered operations, there also follows the question: What about the teacher union? So striking is the dichotomy between staff and administration—i.e., labor and management—in some school districts that the first thought upon introducing any strategy that seeks to have administrators and teachers work together toward some common goal is not, Will the strategy work?, but rather, What will the union say? This outlook is unfortunate.

Throughout this book, it will be consistently repeated that the best working and most productive relationship in the educational sense is a colleagial one in which staff and administration work together to solve problems that affect both groups. Staff involvement does not need to result in nor is it intended to create "management by committee." It is not an attempt to foist administrative burdens onto the shoulders of already overworked staff members. Rather, it is a way to create greater rapport between staff and administration by fostering broader understanding and building a sense of the academic community.

Many school districts already practice the techniques of staff involvement described in this book. Others implement some of the practices. Still others would like to do so. The heart of the problem is

---

[*]Gail Linnea Thierbach, "Decision Involvement and Job Satisfaction in Middle and Junior High Schools," (unpublished paper), University of Wisconsin–Madison, 1980.

change: moving from one mode of operation (noninvolvement or limited staff involvement) to another (greater involvement).

Change is always resisted. It is human nature to prefer the familiar to the unknown, even when the familiar is uncomfortable or ineffective and the unknown promises to be better. Thus, whatever the change may be, some staff members and administrators will oppose it simply because it represents a departure from the known situation.

HOW TO OVERCOME RESISTANCE TO CHANGE

What can progressive school leaders do to overcome this resistance to introducing greater staff involvement in the school management function?

First, at the administrative level, the chief administrator should examine and explain to subordinate administrators what forms of staff involvement are planned and how these techniques will be carried out. To what extent will the staff involvement strategies affect the present work of other administrators? What administrator attitudes need to be considered?

Thorough in-service work at the administrative level is essential to any smooth implementation of management innovations. Whether staff involvement strategies are introduced at the district or building level, responsible administrators seeking to introduce changes will do so only after consulting with their administrative peers and subordinates—e.g., superintendent with support personnel, such as curriculum supervisors; principals with assistant principals, deans, and so on.

Second, the administrator will need to approach staff leaders, such as teacher union officers and representatives. In-service work with key staff should begin at the leadership level so that staff leaders are familiar with the proposed innovations and can transmit that understanding to their colleagues.

By eliciting staff understanding initially at the teacher's union level, less resistance will be encountered later at the general staff level. Most union leaders will recognize staff involvement as a method of encouraging greater teacher self-determination in colleagial atmosphere, where working together with the administration benefits everyone concerned.

BE AWARE OF CONTRACTUAL MATTERS

An area of special awareness for both the administration and teachers will be the contractual agreement between the board of education and the teacher's union. Staff involvement will in no instance contravene contractual agreements, nor will such involvement be used to take the place of normal contract bargaining. Without such an understanding, serious problems will arise when contract and staff involvement outcomes fail to agree.

Yet greater staff involvement is also likely to influence future contractual agreements. A positive outcome of increased staff participation is the increased understanding it brings. Administrators gain insights into the problems and limitations of their teachers, while teachers enlarge their viewpoints to see more clearly the challenges and problems facing their administrators. These insights cannot help but influence future contract negotiations. Usually, the heightened mutual understanding helps to bring teachers and administrators closer together, thus making the bargaining process more open to compromise and understanding.

Staff involvement should hold no threat for anyone who is honestly concerned about improving intraschool human relations. Staff involvement is not about power (i.e., who decides what), but rather about progress—progress toward understanding and unity by which administrators, teachers, and students directly benefit in the educational process.

Donovan R. Walling

About This Book

If you are like most educators, you have spent many frustrating hours in meetings that seemed purposeless and on committees that accomplished little or nothing. Work groups that simply don't work are the bane of education.

Whether you are a superintendent, a principal or assistant principal, a curriculum supervisor, a department head, or if ever you have the job of forming groups of people to work together, this book can help you.

How to Build Staff Involvement in School Management is a practical, how-to guide to organizing individuals into *working* groups. Just a few of the topics covered are:

- How to decide when and why to form a committee.
- How to establish realistic goals and priorities.
- How to develop an effective task force.
- How to use the concept of *shared responsibility* to get results.
- How to foster feelings of "ownership."
- How to design successful plans of operation.
- How to gather needed information effectively.
- How to make staff meetings meaningful.
- How to keep advisory boards on-task and on-target.
- How to develop in-service seminars and workshops that really work.

The book also provides specific suggestions for vital group activities, such as processing ideas, building "community," forming communications links, identifying individual roles, building work skills, and evaluating and refining group structures.

Each chapter contains checklists, charts, examples, diagrams, and illustrations to give you the ammunition you need *now* to make the next committee or task force you form a group that stays on target and gets the job done.

Part One, "School Work Groups: Form and Function," deals with broad patterns of organizational and functional details that apply to most work group situations. Specifically, Chapters One and Two delve into the workings of the committee and its alter ego, the task force. Since many staff work groups fall into one of these two categories, it is appropriate to begin an examination of staff involvement from this point. Chapters Three through Six build upon the basics of group work, presenting ways to develop ownership and responsibility, techniques for assessing needs and gathering information, and plans for organizing and maintaining records. Chapter Six focuses directly on personal presentation skills that every group leader or coordinator needs to work effectively with peer and professional groups and with the public in general.

Part Two, "Staff Involvement: Traditions and Innovations," looks at several specific work groups. These include the staff or faculty meeting, advisory board, quality circle, in-service seminar, and workshop. Each is discussed in a separate chapter devoted to examining the inner workings of these traditional and innovative types of school work groups.

Chapter Twelve introduces a new concept that is making headway in several school districts. The notion of *shared governance* goes beyond staff involvement to include community members and others in the school management function.

Three appendices are also included to provide additional resources: Appendix A, "A Short Glossary of Terms," serves as a compendium of specific management concepts and related terms as they are used in the context of staff involvement. Appendix B, "An Easy Guide to Proper Meeting Procedures," reviews standard rules of order and provides important tips for keeping meetings moving productively. Appendix C, "Selected Resources," provides an assortment of reference books that may be helpful in further developing staff involvement strategies.

Experience has shown that aimless and ineffective groups do more than simply fail to accomplish meaningful goals. They also breed frustration, lower staff morale, and reduce feelings of job satisfaction among group participants. Moreover, unsatisfactory group experiences set a negative tone for the future and make it harder to achieve success in later groups.

Breaking the pattern of failure can only be accomplished by organizing groups that support their individual members while providing clear, positive direction to the whole group. This book shows you the way to success through strategies that have been tried and proven successful.

In short, *How to Build Staff Involvement in School Management* gives school leaders the foundation needed to increase staff involvement through direct, down-to-earth organizational strategies that will fundamentally and positively affect the way your school functions— and succeeds!

Acknowledgments

Over the past several years, I have been able to work with many fine educators whose interests and ideas have both directly and indirectly contributed to the material in this book.

I am grateful for the encouragement received from James Arentsen, principal of Farnsworth Junior High School in Sheboygan, Wisconsin, and from Dr. Richard Penkava, principal of Zweibruecken American High School in West Germany. Thank-you's (if somewhat belated) must also go to several colleagues in Wisconsin: Linda Helf, former president of the Manitowoc Education Association; and Dee Mateer and Wayne Homstad, both former chief negotiators for the Sheboygan Education Association.

Gratitude must also be extended to Dr. Marlin Tanck, Director of Instruction for the Sheboygan Area School District, who made it possible for me to administer an innovative project in gifted education; Gerald DeAmico, a long-time friend and colleague who succeeded me as project administrator; and Norman Heitzman, currently assistant principal at Mannheim American School, who was responsible for a gifted program I was privileged to coordinate during its initial phase.

Thanks also go to Dr. James S. Bonner, Director of Special Education for the Muskegon, Michigan Public Schools, who provided valuable insights into the use of quality circles in education.

Finally, a special vote of thanks must go to my good friend and colleague Jim Burns, whose encouragement and goodwill over many years helped spur this book along. A conscientious and concerned educator, it is to Jim that this book is dedicated.

Contents

Chapter Three

Chapter Four

Chapter Five

Chapter Six

Chapter Ten
Developing Effective Staff Training Seminars 139

Chapter Eleven
Planning Workshops That Work 153

Chapter Twelve
Beyond Staff Involvement: Exploring the Concept
of Shared Governance 165

Part One

SCHOOL WORK GROUPS: FORM AND FUNCTION

- The Committee—Developing a Workable Group
- Structuring Teams and Task Forces
- Creating Links of Responsibility
- Gathering Staff Input Efficiently
- How to Simplify and Systematize Your Recordkeeping and Reporting
- Building Personal Presentation Skills

The Committee—
Developing a
Workable Group

1

COMMITTEES exist in every school, and are a necessary and useful form of group organization. But what exactly is a committee?

A committee is a group of individuals charged with the responsibility of considering and reporting on specific matters relevant to school programs and/or procedures.

Committees are "reactive" rather than "active." This important distinction means that committees are established primarily to react to issues under consideration. A counterpart of the committee, the *task force*, is "active" in the sense of generating or originating new plans and policies. (Task-force operation is discussed in Chapter Two.)

This distinction between a committee and a task force is important in understanding the structure of the committee as a working group.

AIMING FOR PRODUCTIVE OUTCOMES

School committees can be classified into three types: productive, inconclusive, and nonproductive/counterproductive.

Productive committees begin with realistic goals that are specifically defined and systematically accomplished. These are the workhorse groups of a school that provide the direction and insight essential to administrative planning and functioning. The accomplishments of these committees also provide positive feedback to the participants, thereby serving to strengthen staff cohesiveness and morale and to heighten individual job satisfaction.

Inconclusive committees fall short of being productive in that their goals are less distinct. These committees provide discussion forums for current school issues or problems, but tend not to resolve such problems. If a venting of frustration or an exchange of views is all that is needed and is accomplished in a positive vein, inconclusive committees may be appropriate and may even enhance morale, or at least keep it from deteriorating. However, these nebulous sorts of groups run the risk of degenerating into "gripe sessions," which are nonproductive at best.

Nonproductive committees have no goals or have goals that are so vaguely defined or all-encompassing as to be impossible to accomplish. These committees are nonproductive because they reach no positive end. Failure to achieve results often leads to more serious problems, such as lowered staff morale, individual frustration, and negative attitudes toward the committee topic, committee members, the administration, and the system as a whole. In short, these committees become *counterproductive* because the consequences often impact negatively on future staff relations.

The primary focus of this chapter is the successful development of the most effective of these committee types, the productive committee. To create this ideal committee, it will be important to answer systematically the following basic questions:

1. When is it appropriate to form a committee? When would an alternative form of group organization be preferable?
2. How should the committee be structured in order to reach its goals? Do different types of goals require different group structures?
3. Who should participate in the committee? What criteria are used to select participants?
4. How does a committee begin to function—what gets the ball rolling, so to speak?
5. Why is it important for the committee to establish secondary goals and priorities?
6. How can the committee successfully process ideas and synthesize information?

WHEN AND WHEN NOT TO FORM A COMMITTEE

Because a committee's productivity hinges on its results, the criteria for deciding when to form a committee must naturally focus on broad group goals or tasks. Figure 1-1 provides several sample goals.

Task or Goal	Yes	No
A. Review science textbooks to decide future purchases.	X	
B. Revise classroom tardiness policy to incorporate recent court decisions.	X	
C. Develop a plan for a mentor program for gifted students.		X
D. Develop a position statement regarding potential censorship of library materials.	X	
E. Compile a catalog of computer resources in area libraries.		X
F. Explore techniques for teaching nonprint journalism.		X

FIGURE 1-1. Is a Committee the Appropriate Group to Tackle These Problems?

Items A, B, and D in Figure 1-1 are appropriate committee tasks. Reviewing textbooks and other instructional materials, revising existing school policies such as those pertaining to attendance and punctuality, and considering current issues with the goal of taking a stance are reasonable group objectives, fully in keeping with the organizational scope of a committee.

Item C, developing plans for a mentor program, is more appropriately the job of a task force; the goal calls for generating a new program as opposed to reviewing an existing program, and by definition, a task force may originate new programs and procedures.

Item E, compiling a catalog of computer resources in area libraries, is also an undertaking more suited to a task force. Here, teams from within the committee may be utilized to produce the new catalog (see Chapter Two).

Item F, exploring techniques for teaching nonprint journalism, is essentially a learning task. Neither a committee nor a task force is appropriate to this goal. Rather, a learning objective may be dealt with better through some form of in-service training, such as a staff seminar (see Chapter Ten) or a workshop (see Chapter Eleven).

Once it has been determined that the task or goal can be handled within the definition and scope of a committee, the actual group framework must be constructed. Six factors apply, as summarized in the checklist shown in Figure 1-2.

---

1. Is there a deadline for completion of the committee's work?
2. Are the time constraints reasonable?
3. Are qualified staff members willing to serve on the committee?
4. Are the material resource needs known and are resources available?
5. Are support services (research, clerical aid) available, if needed?
6. Is expert assistance available?

FIGURE 1-2. Group Framework Factors

If the answer to each of the questions in Figure 1-2 is "yes," a productive committee can be formed. Otherwise, the "no" responses may indicate potential problems that may result in a nonworkable group. Again, the danger is not merely nonproductivity but counterproductivity, where morale suffers and future committee efforts may be seriously undermined.

DESIGNING COMMITTEE STRUCTURES

Organizational structure takes its impetus from the nature of the committee's task or goal. Simple reviews will lend themselves to small, informal committee structures, but complex, multifaceted problems will require more elaborate organization.

Three organizational models, increasing in structural complexity, are effective for a variety of goals.

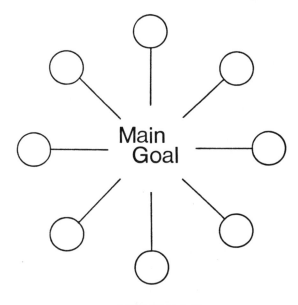

FIGURE 1-3

Figure 1-3 illustrates a circular model. This structure is appropriate when the committee involves only three to eight persons and when the goal of the committee is relatively simple and straightforward.

The action of this form of committee focuses on group discussion, so it is suitable for a small group working toward a central goal. A sample goal from the chart in Figure 1-1, developing a position statement regarding potential censorship of library materials, is an example of the kind of single-dimensional task that is best suited to the circular model.

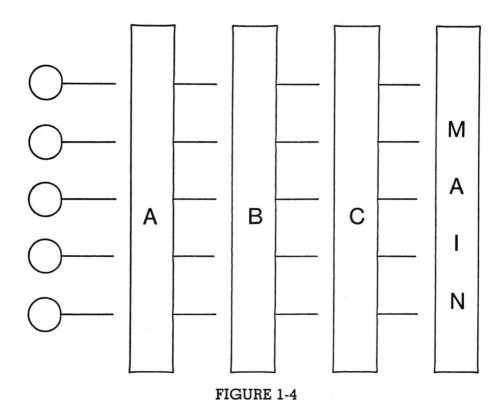

FIGURE 1-4

Figure 1-4 shows the structure of a linear committee model. This form of committee is efficient for goals that must be achieved on a whole group basis but through a series of preliminary stages, or subgoals. Again using the example from Figure 1-1 of revising a classroom tardiness policy to incorporate recent court decisions, some of the stages might be determined as follows:

SUBGOAL A—Review current tardiness policy.

SUBGOAL B—Examine court decisions that apply to school attendance.

SUBGOAL C—Review policies for tardiness in use in other area schools.

MAIN GOAL—Revise classroom tardiness policy.

The linear model, like the circular model, is intended for groups with fewer than ten members. The advantage of the linear model is its ability to process systematically more complex tasks.

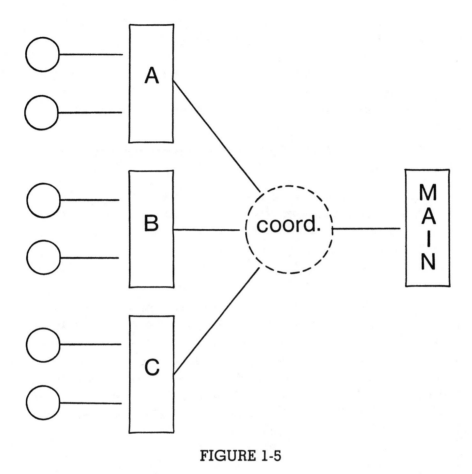

FIGURE 1-5

Figure 1-5 illustrates the most complex organizational model, a modular structure. In this form, the committee can subdivide into small groups, thereby breaking down a multifaceted task into logical and more workable components. Each unit, or subcommittee, works independently from the other units toward completion of its goal. Then the various unit responses are funneled through a coordinator (or coordinating group) to reach the main goal of the total committee.

A subcommittee should consist of only two or three individuals. These participants are charged with specific responsibilities that contribute to the total group decision-making process. The modular committee structure, utilizing two or more subcommittees, can be particularly helpful when the main goal of the total committee hinges on consideration of a wide variety of information. For example, when a committee goal is to review science textbooks for future purchase selections in several disciplines, it facilitates the decision process to have the various discipline specialists review potential texts for their own subject areas. In this way, individual expertise can best contribute to the total group process.

A final example from Figure 1-1 shows the workings of the modular structure:

GROUP A GOAL—Review textbooks for general science.

GROUP B GOAL—Review textbooks for chemistry.

GROUP C GOAL— Review textbooks for biology.

Group decisions are transmitted to the coordinator, perhaps the science department head, who assembles the overall committee conclusion.

MAIN GOAL—Review science textbooks to determine future purchases.

Modular organization units allow a larger number of participants and more specialized participation. However, there is a note of caution to be observed. Very large committees can become so fragmented that the process of coordination becomes overwhelming. In cases where the goal is extremely complex, foresight will enable the task to be divided among two or three committees, each with its own subcommittees. This division of labor is preferable to a single, unmanageably complex "monster" committee.

Understanding that there is a variety of committee models can help committee participants and leaders to choose the organizational form that best matches the task at hand. Here's a quick reference chart:

```
Small Group  +  Simple Goal   =  Circular Model
Small Group  +  Complex Goal  =  Linear Model
Large Group  +  Complex Goal  =  Modular Model
```

WHO PARTICIPATES AND WHY

Many school committees are made up of volunteer participants and, by and large, this is the preferred method of committee formation. Self-selection to a committee, rather than assignment, tends to ensure that committee work gets off on a positive footing. On the other hand, unless potential difficulties are recognized and avoided, this method may cause some problems. For example:

- Self-selection may result in too many or too few participants.
- Self-selection does not assure that participants will have needed knowledge or skills appropriate to the committee task.
- Self-selection may pose problems with scheduling because of diverse commitments among participants.

Successfully avoiding these and similar problems is relatively easy. Most selection difficulties stem from lack of understanding about the task and goal of the committee. Inappropriate self-selection can be reduced by providing more complete information about the committee prior to the selection process. Figure 1-6 shows an information sheet containing the items necessary for intelligent self-selection.

Note the kinds of information supplied in this sample: what the committee is supposed to do, when the committee's meeting schedule will start and when the goal should be reached, when individual meetings begin—and end—and where, how many participants are needed and what skills or knowledge they should possess, who to contact in order to volunteer, and when the contact must be made. By providing this basic information in a staff flyer or bulletin board posting, the committee head can reasonably expect that qualified staff members who have an interest in the committee's topic will volunteer to participate.

Naturally, if this form of committee making is new to the staff, some preliminary explanation will be necessary. However, once this technique is adopted—provided that it is used consistently—most staff members will respond positively.

There may be two complications:

1. What if too few individuals volunteer?
2. What if too many volunteer?

If there are too few volunteers, some further investigation is needed. Is the committee really needed? Does the topic truly concern staff members, or should the matter be handled by the administration? If the committee's goal is viable (meaning that it really does concern the staff), perhaps the problem lies in the schedule. Are meeting times inconvenient? Too frequent? Or, is the problem one of qualifications; are they too narrow, for instance?

Sometimes a simple change is all that is required to make the committee workable. Conducting this type of investigation, and finding

Committee Title:

Tardiness Policy Revision Committee

Goal:

To revise the current school tardiness policy in order to incorporate recent court decisions.

First Meeting:

Monday, January 14, 19—
3:30–4:30 P.M.
Room 304

Anticipated Meeting Schedule:

Mondays and Thursdays, 3:30–4:30 P.M.

Completion Deadline:

March 1, 19—

Number of Participants Needed:

6–8

Skills/Knowledge Required:

Understanding of current attendance/tardiness policy.

Skills/Knowledge Desired:

A. Knowledge of current legal decisions in the area of school attendance/tardiness.
B. Knowledge of policies regarding attendance and tardiness in other area schools.

Contact Person:

Mr. John Stewart, Principal

Contact Deadline:

January 7, 19—

FIGURE 1-6. Committee Information Sheet

out more about staff concerns in systematic and meaningful ways, is dealt with in detail in Chapter Three.

Too many volunteers is a less serious problem in most instances. It is most important that personalities not become a factor in the selection process. The key to choosing among volunteers is *objectivity*. The skills and knowledge qualifications of the volunteers must serve as effective selection tools. Where qualifications are equal, it may be necessary to reexamine the desired skills and knowledge areas to make them more specific. Or, given equal qualifications, it may be desirable to devise a simple lottery system to select committee participants in a nonjudgmental fashion.

ORIENTING THE COMMITTEE COMPASS

The committee foundation provided by the initial information— as outlined in Figure 1-6—must be immediately expanded at the outset by a firm understanding of the group's *level of authority*.

To function competently, committee participants need to know the degree of impact their considerations and conclusions will have on management operation. Essentially, will committee results serve as (a) information, (b) recommendation, or (c) decision?

These three levels of authority determine much of the tenor of the committee.

1. Information

This is the lowest level of authority. Committee results at this level are used as basic data for external decision making by others, such as the principal, the department head, or the subject matter specialist.

2. Recommendation

At this middle level of authority, committee work produces both information and suggestions for appropriate actions or decisions.

3. Decision

This is the highest level of authority. Here, committee work draws conclusions and *makes decisions* that are to be implemented by school officials.

Participants' knowledge and acceptance of the committee's level of authority are crucial to success. Trust and cooperation between committee participants and the committee supervisor—i.e., the person to whom the committee reports, not necessarily the committee head—depend on the participants' understanding of the group's task or goal and on the extent to which their work will direct or dictate a future response by the supervising authority.

Different expectations are encountered, depending on the level of authority; those expectations may influence the supervisor's choice of the committee's level of authority.

The information level of authority creates the fewest expectations. Committee participants understand that their deliberations are to provide information, ideas, data, and so on. This form of committee is least restrictive to the initiatives of the supervisor, since his or her subsequent actions are in no way constrained by the work of the committee, and he or she may use the committee findings in whatever manner is deemed appropriate. This factor may be a distinct plus in some cases. But there are also limitations to the information level of authority. For instance, it is essential that the committee's work be important in the eyes of the participants. A goal or task that is viewed as trivial will result in either initially few participants or subsequently a nonproductive group. In fact, goals that are viewed as unimportant may even produce a committee that is counterproductive.

The recommendation level of the committee may relieve the committee supervisor of the responsibility of some aspects of decision making, thus making his or her job easier. At the same time, the supervisor is not bound to accept the committee's recommendation. Therein lies the potential problem. Given the authority to recommend sometimes translates in the minds of individual committee members into an expectation that the recommendation will be accepted—i.e., that a decision has been made. To avoid this problem, it is essential that committee members understand that a recommendation may be accepted or rejected based on other factors that weigh into the final decision. The clarity of this understanding will ultimately determine how committee members and supervisors feel about the work they do on the committee and the way in which their recommendations are handled.

The decision level relieves the supervisor of both the opportunity and the responsibility for making a final decision. In many instances, management is reluctant to allow committees to function at this level of authority because the committee, for all practical purposes, "becomes" management. Not only may this situation be uncomfortable for the supervisor, but it may also place too great a psychological burden on committee members. If, however, the committee is structured to make decisions, the supervisor should not interfere with or attempt to influence its decisions. Once granted the authority to make decisions, the committee must be allowed to exercise that authority.

The question for the supervisor often boils down to: Am I willing to accept the decision of the committee? If the answer is *no*, the committee must be informed that its final product will be used for information only, or that its recommendations will be sought and considered but also weighed against other factors.

Nothing so frustrates and angers committee members as to work under the false assumption—or, worse, a false set of instructions—that they are to arrive at a decision and then to find that that decision has been overturned or rejected. When this problem arises, the consequences are invariably negative and often far-reaching.

"Orienting the committee compass" in this regard is sufficient reason to spend some time in in-service activities that develop staff members' awareness of the nature of committees and their levels of authority. A further step might then be taken to inform prospective committee members fully about the authority level of a committee by placing this information directly on the information sheet that announces the group's formation.

Before incorporating the level of authority on the information sheet, however, make sure that staff members understand the terminology. As pointed out earlier, while the definition of a *recommendation* is seemingly clear, experience has shown that it too often connotes a degree of acceptance that may, in fact, not be present.

Various forms of in-service training procedures are developed in later chapters.

ESTABLISHING GOALS AND PRIORITIES

Most committees will need to establish a series of subgoals or specific objectives as steps, or stages, in working toward their main goals. Likewise, it will be necessary to place these specific objectives into some logical order, so that one objective leads sequentially to the next.

Figure 1-7 asks a series of questions that will be helpful in identifying and delineating specific subgoals.

After appropriate subgoals have been characterized, they should be ordered for efficient handling. Placing ideas into a priority sequence is an important initial consideration of the new committee.

Figure 1-8 again asks a series of questions that will help you establish committee priorities.

1. What information is necessary before the main goal can be approached?
2. Are preliminary decisions needed before the main task of the committee can be tackled?
3. Are committee participants sufficiently informed?
4. Should the main goal be clarified further in order to "fine tune" the committee's efforts?
5. What form will the committee's results take?
6. Are identified subgoals stated in clear, behavioral terms?
7. Does each subgoal single out a particular task or idea, rather than jumbling several, possibly conflicting ideas or chores together?

FIGURE 1-7. Goal Development

In ordering the work of the committee, a good rule of thumb is to adapt the well-known journalists' axiom of *5 W's and H*:

- *What* is the job of the committee?
- *Who* can do that job best?
- *When* will the work take place?
- *Where* will the committee meet?

1. Does each subgoal fit into the overall design, so that committee work flows logically toward the main goal?
2. Is each subgoal suited to the time allotment?
3. Has consideration been given to any special preparation needed to meet each subgoal?
4. Will all key questions be answered by the committee's order of work?
5. Is each subgoal really necessary?

FIGURE 1-8. Prioritizing Goals

- *Why* is the committee's task needed?
- *How* will the committee's results be used?

If these questions are thoroughly and convincingly answered, it is reasonably assured that the committee's goal is both worthwhile and reachable. And, through systematic accomplishment of well-ordered subgoals, that main goal will be achieved.

PROCESSING IDEAS SUCCESSFULLY

Having spent some time in organizing the goals and priorities of a committee, it is now appropriate to consider how each goal or subgoal is to be achieved. What steps are important in the processing of group ideas in order to reach a synthesis or consensus? Here is a four-stage procedure that works well in the group setting:

STAGE ONE—Goal Stating

What is the goal? Does each committee member understand the objective of the group? Can the task of the group be clearly and simply stated? What is the central "question" or "problem"?

STAGE TWO—Option Finding

What are the options that answer the question? Which options are similar? Compatible? Conflicting? What background, reasoning, or research gives each option its credibility?

STAGE THREE—Decision Making

Which option provides the most suitable solution to the question or problem? Can several options be synthesized? Is it really necessary to settle on only one option?

STAGE FOUR—Evaluation

Is the decision appropriate to the main goal of the committee? What impact does the decision have on succeeding subgoals? Earlier decisions? Given the constraints of the task, is the decision (product) valid?

By using this step-by-step procedure, group decisions can be reached in a systematic and effective manner. One note, however, is additionally valuable: In the words of an old song, "Accentuate the positive." Looking for negative solutions gains nothing and wastes time. It may be interesting, even intriguing, to consider what won't work, but the key to a successful committee is to focus on what *will* work—to find a positive answer that meets the committee goal.

SIX KEYS TO EFFECTIVE COMMITTEES

1. Make sure the committee has a definite goal. Productive committees are more than useful; they achieve meaningful ends.

2. Understand which goals are appropriate to the committee structure and which might be better suited to other organizational forms.

3. Provide solid support. Be certain that the committee has the time, resources, and administrative support that it needs to function effectively.

4. Choose the committee form that fits the task. Avoid unnecessary complications.

5. Provide sound start-up information. Potential committee participants need to know what they will be expected to do. And they will need to know what authority their work will carry.

6. Recognize committee accomplishments by using the committee's results appropriately.

This last key is one that deserves particular emphasis. Not only should the group's results be used as they were intended to be used, but the individual participants themselves deserve recognition for a job well done. Recognition is important to the individual's self-esteem, morale, and sense of job satisfaction. Opportunities should be taken to provide suitable rewards, such as spotlighting the group's efforts at a public meeting of the board of education or at the next faculty meeting. Individual letters of appreciation are another way of rewarding committee service. Additional ideas for building staff morale through recognition and rewards are specifically detailed in Chapter Three.

By utilizing the six keys listed above, school leaders can ensure that they develop workable groups that are organized to be effective.

Structuring Teams and Task Forces

2

MUCH of the information given in Chapter One applies equally to the committee's counterpart, the task force. The differences between the two organizational structures stem not from their essential form, but rather from the ends toward which the group is directed.

In a very real sense, the task force is the committee's alter ego.

In Chapter One, a committee was defined as "a group of individuals charged with the responsibility of considering and reporting on specific matters" of consequence to the school. As the definition and functions of the committee were developed, it became clear that the committee's role is "reactive" in nature; i.e., committees are formed for the purpose of reviewing such matters as administrative policy, procedure, and the like. Committees are not responsible for generating new policies.

Here, then, is a working definition of the school task force:

A task force is a group of individuals charged with the responsibility of developing new policies, programs, plans, or procedures in matters relevant to the school.

EXPLORING ALTERNATIVES TO THE COMMITTEE FORM

Too often, all school or school system work groups are lumped together under the heading of *committees.* Consequently, goals and objectives become muddled and both supervisors and participants are prone to lose sight of their distinct roles in the conflicting functions of different types of "committees." More narrowly defining the term *committee* and developing compatible partner forms—e.g., the task force, the team—helps to avoid this potential confusion.

Where the role of the committee was characterized as reporting, reviewing, and revising, the role of the task force may be summarized as defining, developing, and deciding.

Let's explore each of these new elements.

Defining Direction

The first job of any task force is to define the focus and direction of its activities. Like the committee, the task force must begin by defining its goals. Unlike the committee, the task force's charge may be more open-ended. Characteristically, the chores assigned to task forces tend to be less finite than those given to committees. The act of generating something new is less restrictive than the act of reviewing something already in service.

Developing Approach

Once the goal of the task force is defined, the next stage is to develop an approach or several approaches to that goal. Here, as with the committee, it will be necessary to consider group structures in relation to the specific goal. Some concrete examples will be dealt with later in this chapter.

Reaching a Conclusion

Finally, it will fall to the task force to reach a conclusion. This conclusion may take the form of a new policy, a set of procedures, a plan for implementation, or some other new "product."

Again, there is a parallel with the committee in that the decisions reached by the task force are also governed by the level of authority at which the group has been instructed to operate. The task force's conclusions may merely provide information or recommendations, or they may indeed form management decisions. For a fuller discussion of these levels of authority, see the section entitled "Orienting the Committee Compass" in Chapter One.

While it should be noted that there are fundamental similarities between the committee and the task force, there are also some significant differences. These differences and their importance to building staff involvement in school management will become clearer as we examine further the nature and workings of the task force.

REFINING GROUP STRUCTURES

It will be helpful to examine a task force in action to understand more fully the workings of this type of group. Let's take the example of an elementary school faculty which has been called upon to develop a program for gifted and talented students in their school. An information sheet for the task force follows the same pattern as shown in Figure 1-6. It is illustrated in Figure 2-1.

The information sheet generates nine volunteers as follows:

Ms. Swanson—Kindergarten

Mrs. Smith—Grade 1

Mr. Lawrence—Grade 2

Ms. Judson—Grade 3

Mrs. Frank—Grade 3

Mr. Everett—Grade 4

Mrs. Lloyd—Grade 4

Ms. Johnson—Grade 6

Mr. Hart—Grade 6

Since Grade 5 is not represented in the volunteer list, the task force's head approaches one of the fifth-grade teachers, Mr. Perth, who subsequently joins the group. The total task force now consists of eleven individuals, including the head who will serve in an active role as a participant.

Using the models provided in Chapter One for organizational structure (Figures 1-3, 1-4, and 1-5), it becomes clear that the task force must adopt the modular model because of the multifaceted nature of the task. Working as a total group, the participants define their subgoals as follows:

1. Survey current literature in order to become familiar with various types of gifted education programs.

2. Investigate forms of identification.

3. Determine local resources for an elementary gifted and talented program.

In order to meet the subgoals, the group is divided into three teams.

Task Force Title:

Gifted and Talented Program Development Task Force

Goal:

To develop a multiphase program for gifted and talented students in grades K–6, including identification and treatment procedures.

First Meeting:

Tuesday, November 1, 19__
3:15–4:00 P.M.
Instructional Materials Center

Anticipated Meeting Schedule:
Tuesdays, weekly, 3:15–4:00 P.M.

Completion Deadline:

June 1, 19__

Number of Participants Needed:

7 or more (at least one per grade level, K–6)

Skills/Knowledge Required:

No special requirement.

Skills/Knowledge Desired:

Understanding of current trends in gifted education.

Level of Authority:

Recommendation.

Contact Person:

Mrs. Larson, Media Specialist

Contact Deadline:

October 22, 19__

FIGURE 2-1. Gifted Task Force Information Sheet

TEAMS OR TASK FORCE?
A QUESTION OF NEED

In task force terms, a *team* is the counterpart of a subcommittee. It consists of two or three persons focused on a single task or goal.

In the example of the elementary gifted education program, the multifaceted nature of the main goal makes it imperative that the total task force be split into various teams in order to approach more logically and efficiently the identified subgoals.

Where the main goal is less broad, the entire task force may function better as a single unit, following the plan outlined in the circular and linear models discussed earlier.

For the example, the following teams are designated by the task force leader, Mrs. Larson:

Team A

Ms. Swanson (K)

Mr. Lawrence (2)

Mrs. Lloyd (4)

Mr. Hart (6)

Team A's task will be to research the literature to survey the various forms of gifted education and report back to the group through the coordinating team.

Team B

Mrs. Smith (1)

Ms. Judson (3)

Mr. Everett (4)

Miss Johnson (6)

Team B's task will be to investigate various methods of identifying students for potential inclusion in the new program.

Team C

Mrs. Frank (3)

Mr. Perth (5)

Mrs. Larson (Media Specialist)

Team C's task will be to examine local resources as possible aids for the new program.

The coordinating team is also formed and consists of one member from each of the other teams—for instance, Mr. Lawrence, Miss Johnson, and the task force leader, Mrs. Larson. The role of this team is to collect information, summarize and synthesize as needed, and distribute it to the total group.

Some effort should be made to keep each team as representative as possible of the total group. Since the task force was designed to operate on a K–6 basis, each team includes a variety of grade levels. This variety serves several purposes:

- It allows for diversity of experience.
- It promotes a "whole picture" view of the given task.
- It helps to encourage on-task discussion rather than mere shop talk.

The male-female diversity of the total group is also maintained in the smaller teams to the extent possible. This awareness, too, contributes to the purposes above.

The teams also take into consideration the desired skills and knowledge mentioned on the information sheet. For example, Mr. Lawrence is placed on Team A, which is conducting the literature search, because he recently took a college course in which he wrote a paper on gifted education. His background knowledge will help further the team's work. Likewise, the task force leader Mrs. Larson's job as a media specialist makes her an excellent choice for the team charged with determining local resources that may be available for the new program.

USING "SHARED RESPONSIBILITY"

Shared responsibility means that the task of working toward a specified goal is a group commitment, not merely an individual responsibility. It will be observed that even the subgroups (teams in the case of a task force, subcommittees in the case of a committee) are always composed of two or more persons. The reason for this goes beyond the old adage that "two heads are better than one." Sharing responsibility for achieving a goal brings with it these advantages over individual efforts:

- Mutual support, both physically in terms of carrying the workload and psychologically in terms of encouragement.

- Diversity of viewpoints, experience, insights, and concerns that give greater depth and breadth to the group's work.

- Internal evaluation—group members help one another to recognize flaws and weaknesses that might otherwise be overlooked.

- Opportunities to use special individual talents—i.e., playing to personal strengths of individual group members.

- Learning opportunities: younger staff members may learn from older ones and vice versa; experienced faculty provide examples for less experienced members.

All of these are excellent reasons for adopting the concept of shared responsibility.

AN EXAMPLE OF A TASK FORCE IN ACTION

To finish with the example of the elementary gifted education program, it will be easiest to look at the task force's operation in the form of a flow chart. A step-by-step description of the work of the group is shown in Figure 2-2.

The flow of information illustrated in Figure 2-2 is direct and simple. It shows how most task forces using a modular organizational structure can and do operate. However, variations and elaborations are both feasible and sometimes desirable. For example, if the goal of the task force is more complex, it will be necessary to provide for greater give and take between individual teams and the whole task force. Figure 2-2 provides for essentially a one-way flow of information, always proceeding toward the final goal in a direct manner. This directness is not always possible. A more complex goal may create the need for feedback as, likewise, such a need may result from a larger number of participants on the task force.

Figure 2-3 shows a graphic flow chart illustrating the feedback capacity that is inherent in the modular organizational structure.

Information in the diagram flows both from the teams to the coordinator (or coordinating team) and vice versa, and from the coordinator to the whole task force and vice versa. In all instances, the information flow passes through the coordinating function, which is essential to clear communication. Since it is the role of the coordinator to tie everything together, random communication should be eschewed in favor of more structured give and take.

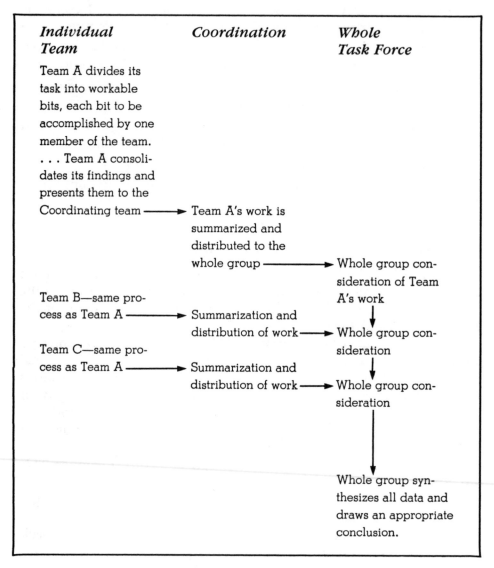

FIGURE 2-2. Activity Flow Chart

TASK FORCE AS LINKED TEAMS

In some instances, it may be preferable to use a variation of the linear model instead of the modular organizational structure because the subgoals are sequential rather than independent. For example, the task force may feel that it would be better to know about gifted programs

Teams

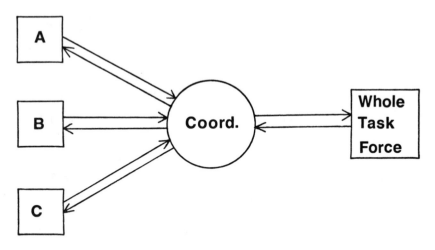

FIGURE 2-3

described in current educational literature (subgoal 1) *before* investigating forms of identification of potential gifted students (subgoal 2).

However, the linear model shown in Figure 1-4 provides for the whole task force to work sequentially through a series of subgoals. For larger groups or for groups whose members can devote only a limited amount of time to the task force project, this linear structure may prove inefficient. If so, an alternative is possible in the form of *linked teams.*

In a linked team concept, Team A completes its work toward its assigned subgoal, then passes along its results to Team B. Team B considers Team A's work and proceeds toward its own assigned subgoal, handing on its results to Team C, and so on. The last team's work passes eventually to the whole task force, which serves as a reviewing body.

The linked team concept is illustrated in Figure 2-4. This building-block approach offers two distinctions that set it apart from the modular structure: First, it allows each succeeding group to "build" upon the work of earlier groups, unlike the modular approach where each team works independently toward the final review. Second, it allows for minimum involvement of some participants, an advantage where time limitations and crowded work schedules are a factor.

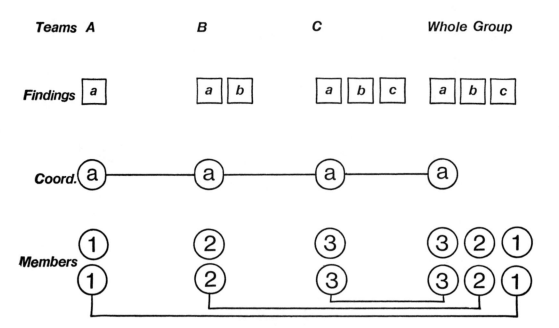

FIGURE 2-4

As shown in the diagram, certain individuals—such as the task force leader—provide continuity to the linked team process by serving on each team. And, all the various participants gather for the whole task force review at the conclusion of the individual teams' efforts.

(It is assumed in this illustration that one or more whole group meetings are conducted at the start of the group process in order to establish goals, guidelines, schedules, and the like.)

Here, then, are some questions to be answered in determining which of the organizational patterns discussed is best suited to the goals and participants involved in the task force.

The answers to the questions in Figure 2-5 will serve as a guide to choosing the most effective group organizational structure for any given task force.

THE ROLE OF THE TASK FORCE LEADER

It is important to recognize the role of the task force leader—and, equally, of the committee head—as one requiring active participation in the group. This is true whether the team leader is the superinten-

---

1. Is the goal of the task force single- or multidimensional?
2. Will subgoals be necessary in order to break up the main goal into workable bits?
3. Are the subgoals independent or interdependent (sequential)?
4. Is the task force group large or small in number?
5. Should the whole task force work together to accomplish the subgoals, or would smaller teams be more efficient?
6. Can participants' individual talents and strengths be used better in the task force as a whole or in the individual teams?
7. Are time and frequency of meetings factors for certain participants?

FIGURE 2-5. Which Structure Is Most Appropriate?

dent or principal, the librarian (recall Mrs. Larson, the media specialist in the gifted program example), a teacher, department head, or curriculum specialist. Each leader must also be a worker. By actively participating in the group, the leader accomplishes several ends:

1. The leader models appropriate behavior for the group effort.
2. The leader monitors group progress and can act accordingly to keep work on target.
3. The leader can provide the "larger viewpoint" when the group breaks into smaller teams or subcommittees.
4. The leader can more readily coordinate concluding activities.
5. The leader provides an individual contribution.

More about leadership and developing staff leaders is contained in later chapters.

THREE ROADS TO RESULTS

Task force effectiveness depends on its qualities of clarity, directness, and closure. These three qualities can be termed "roads to results."

Clarity

Is the goal of the task force clear? Does each member of the total group understand what needs to be accomplished?

A well-defined goal is essential to the functioning of any work group. It is doubly important when the group is designed to create a new program or policy for the school or school district, since inherent in the goal are qualities of feasibility and acceptability. These qualities may be unstated, but they are usually commonly understood as an integral part of understanding the task force goal itself.

If there is any doubt about what will and will not be acceptable as a conclusion, the constraints should be stated at the outset. Much of the frustration that arises when a task force's recommendations are turned down or not implemented stems from lack of understanding of goal constraints.

Goals stated in the clearest manner possible and thoroughly understood by all parties concerned with the task force will ensure that a successful foundation is laid for group work.

Directness

In working toward the task force goal, has the most direct path been chosen? Does the organizational structure of the group suit the task at hand?

Four organizational patterns have been presented for consideration:

The *circular model* is best suited to single-dimensional goals and small task forces. It is based on whole group discussion focused on the main goal.

The *linear model* works well for small task forces that must approach the main goal through the attainment of a series of subgoals. Again, though, it emphasizes whole group activity over smaller teams.

The *linked team* variation of the linear model is more appropriate for larger groups, where smaller teams each take on individual subgoals. Subgoal sequencing is maintained with the first team passing its information on to the second, the second to the third, and so on. Finally, the whole group acts as a review body to summarize and draw conclusions from the teams' efforts.

The *modular model* allows teams to work on independent subgoals, channeling their findings through a coordinator or coordinating group that serves to summarize and synthesize team results for presentation to the task force. In this model, as in a linked team situation, the task force serves as review body.

By choosing the organizational structure that most directly achieves the goal, work time is efficiently used and results are assured within responsible timelines.

Closure

The task force must reach a point of closure. Unlike committees, which are sometimes set up to be self-perpetuating—e.g., standing committees—task forces by definition have a specified end in the form of a new "product" for the school. This goal reaching provides a sense of accomplishment and satisfaction to the participants, and enhances personal job satisfaction.

Several researchers have commented on the importance of closure to individuals' feelings of worth and accomplishment. In building staff involvement in school management, these feelings are valuable considerations. Appropriately handled, the personal, psychological needs of staff members can be satisfied, and greater staff involvement and unity can be developed.

Chapters Three, Four, and Five are devoted to managerial techniques for communication and information processing. These techniques will aid in developing effective work groups of all kinds. Further, Chapter Six provides useful information about personal presentation skills that are valuable to group leaders and coordinators.

The chapters in Part Two demonstrate how committee and task force operations may be put to effective use in a variety of specific group situations. Included are such traditional forms as faculty meetings and in-service training groups, as well as more innovative forms, such as advisory boards and quality circles.

Creating Links of Responsibility

3

WHENEVER school work groups are created, there is a need for clear understanding of both group and individual responsibilities. Understanding responsibility is the key to efficiency and, ultimately, to success.

The essential question is this: *Who* is responsible to *whom* and for *what?*

Answering this question—or, rather, discovering how to answer this question in the context of staff involvement in school management—is the central theme of this chapter. Let's start by defining the *who*'s and the *what*'s of group work.

FOSTERING FEELINGS OF "OWNERSHIP"

First, what is "ownership"?

Ownership can be defined as *proprietorship* and *dominion.* Together the terms imply the qualities of possession and control.

Applied to group work, ownership means that the group deals with a question or problem that in some way *belongs* to the group. Group members have a stake in the problem to be solved, or the goal or task in question.

For example, to use one of the sample goals listed in Figure 1-1, revising a classroom tardiness policy is a problem that belongs to a teacher work group because teachers deal with tardiness on a daily basis. How tardiness is to be handled concerns teachers; therefore, ownership is created through possession of the problem.

The synonym *dominion*, however, implies not only simple possession of the problem, but control as well. In group work, it is essential to initiate and maintain control over the problem and its solution. And, it is in the area of control that a potential new problem may arise, that of control versus authority.

It is essential to effective group work that the concepts of control and authority be separate and distinct. Here are two helpful definitions:

> I. *Control means that the group directs its own work, determining subgoals and priorities, designing an appropriate organizational structure, and reaching conclusions without external process constraints.*

Note the phrase "without external process constraints." Committees, task forces, and other work groups must be free from external constraints that dictate how the group is to function and that rob the group of ownership. At the same time, it should be realized that every group must function within limits: available resources, time and space constraints. These limitations are legitimate and are usually accepted by the group without the concept of ownership being diminished. Time, space, and resource constraints are viewed as "beyond control," and consequently outside the control definition.

> II. *Authority means the level at which the results of the group process are accepted and used to influence or direct management decisions.*

As discussed in Chapter One, a group's conclusions may be used in one of three ways: as *information*, as *recommendation*, or as *decision*. Provided that the group clearly understands its functional level of authority, there is no conflict between control and authority. The way in which a group works (process) is independent of the way in which the results of the work are to be used.

On the other hand, problems will arise if the group's level of authority is unclear. Some groups may feel that if they control the process of their work, they also control the way in which their results will be utilized. For this reason, it is essential that the group's level of authority be known and understood by each member of the work group. This will not only encourage feelings of ownership but also assure a productive group.

Ownership, then, is determined most strongly by the members' familiarity and involvement with the goal or problem (i.e., possession; proprietorship) and by their ability to direct the work process toward a suitable conclusion (i.e., control; dominion).

Group work is most effective when feelings of ownership are

greatest—that is, when group participants have a stake in the task at hand. Here is a checklist for determining ownership:

Given a specific goal to be reached or problem to be solved:

1. Whose problem is it? Who has a vested interest in the goal or solution?

2. Who understands the goal situation—e.g., who has the skills/knowledge to approach the task, or is willing to acquire those needed skills?

3. Who is willing to undertake the job of solving the problem?

FIGURE 3-1. Determining Ownership

Those individuals who "own" the problem, understand how to work toward a solution, and are willing to undertake the task of tackling the problem are the persons best suited to serve in the work group. Their ownership will assure diligence and success better than any other work characteristic.

DESIGNING COMMUNICATION LINKS

Ownership is the unstated motivation for self-selection and the reason that volunteerism is the most effective manner of gathering individuals to work in groups. When self-selection doesn't work, the problem can usually be traced to a problem of ownership.

Proceeding, then, on the basis of a self-selected work group, the next consideration is one of responsible communication. We come back to the "*who* is responsible to *whom*" part of the question asked at the beginning of this chapter.

Within the group, communication links are determined by the nature of the goal or task. As shown in Chapters One and Two, organizational structure is determined by the simplicity or complexity of the task of the group, whether that group is a committee or a task force—or, for that matter, a faculty group meeting as a total staff, an advisory board, a seminar group, or a workshop (all of which are dealt with separately in later chapters). But there are also communication links with the work group supervisor, and between the supervisor and his or her superiors in the school's chain of command.

Figure 3-2 shows a typical chain of communication.

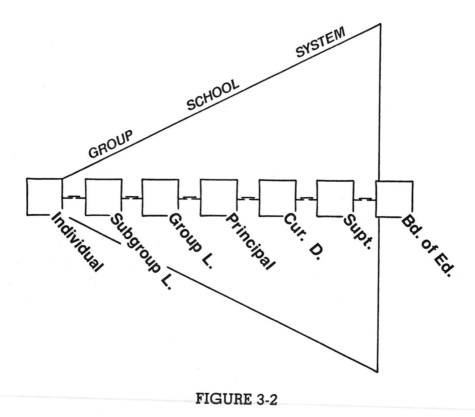

FIGURE 3-2

In this illustration, the full cone of communication can be seen. Beginning with the individual at the cone's tip, communication broadens through successive stages to encompass the subgroup, which is part of the larger work group. That work group, in turn, is a part of the school faculty, which of course is a part of the total school system.

Likewise, the individual links in the chain of communication begin with the individual group (subgroup) member, who is responsible to the subgroup leader/coordinator, who, in turn, is responsible to the group leader. In many instances, the work group leader reports to the building principal. The principal, in turn, reports to the curriculum director, who is responsible to the superintendent. And the superintendent, naturally, is responsible to the board of education.

There is no uniform structure for school systems in the United States, but the chain of communication shown in Figure 3-2 is fairly typical and can be adapted for individual system differences. More important than merely knowing the chain of communication is using that chain.

At the outset of group work, it is a good idea to discuss communication links, so that everyone is aware of the communication chain and how he or she fits into it. Based on the military chain of command, the communication chain is most effective when individual roles within the chain are understood by all concerned, and the chain structure is used to channel communication.

For most individuals within the chain, there are two basic questions to be answered in any group work situation:

1. *Who* is responsible for communicating with me?

2. To *whom* am I responsible for communication?

When these questions are answered, the role of the individual in respect to the group and to the larger school and system will be better understood. The result will be more effective work groups.

USING FLOW CHARTS EFFECTIVELY

Figure 3-2 is an example of a flow chart, in this case illustrating communication flow within a school system.

Flow charts are useful to group work because they show graphically how communication is to be channeled or how work is to be accomplished. They can be used to plan systematically the stages necessary for reaching group goals.

Not all flow charts need to be constructed on paper. Another method that works well is to use a bulletin board card system. An example is shown in Figure 3-3.

This figure illustrates an *action flow chart*. Unlike more traditional flow charts that tend only to show visually the structure of a process or organization, an action flow chart maps out not only what happens but who is responsible, and gives an indication of the time sequence of the process. In a sense, the action flow chart combines some of the characteristics of the traditional flow chart and the timeline.

The simplified example in Figure 3-3 is a portion of an action flow chart that might be used by the task force of linked teams discussed in Chapter Two. Here, Team A is engaged in researching gifted education materials available in local libraries.

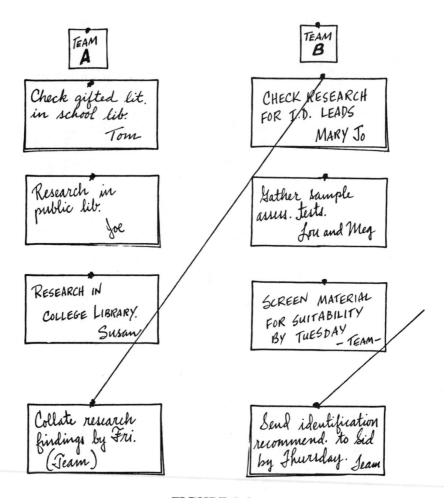

FIGURE 3-3

Team members Tom, Joe, and Susan have given themselves individual assignments that culminate in a whole group review to be conducted by the team "by Friday."

Following the linked team concept, Team A will then hand off its conclusions to one member of Team B, Mary Jo, who will review Team A's work for identification leads to research. At the same time, other members of Team B—Lou and Meg—will be gathering sample assessment tests. "By Tuesday" the whole team will have screened all their material and will be ready to pass on their findings to the next team, represented by Sid in this sample.

Visually charting the progress of ideas and information by means of the action flow chart allows all task force members to view the "total picture" and to understand how they fit into the scheme of communication. And a sense of timelines helps keep the action moving steadily toward resolution of the problem and achievement of the group's main goal.

The card/bulletin board technique is handy for several reasons:

- It's inexpensive and materials are readily available.
- The flow chart can be altered quickly whenever the need arises.
- The large size allows for greater detail and expansion; easier readability.

Some additional tips that may be of value are these:

- Use colored index cards to differentiate among the teams or subcommittees, or to distinguish among various types of actions —for example:
  Red cards for research,
  Blue cards for whole group discussion,
  Orange cards for reports, and so on.
- Attach the card to the bulletin board using a push pin; then illustrate the flow of the chart by connecting the pins with yarn. (Colored yarn may also be used to convey different meanings.)

The action flow chart will improve group efficiency and strengthen communication links. The potential of this simple device is well worth the small effort it will take to construct and maintain the action flow chart.

FORGING CLEAR PATTERNS OF AUTHORITY

The individuals designated in the chain of communication—see Figure 3-2—also represent the line of authority. In developing patterns of authority, the central question is obvious: Who is in charge?

Clearly, the line of authority need not be as long as the one shown in Figure 3-2. For example, the principal may be the group leader, thus eliminating one of the links in the chain. Or, the goal may not need to be split into subgoals; therefore, the subgroups and subgroup leaders are eliminated.

In similar fashion, the chain of communication may be differently structured. While all work groups theoretically fall under the ultimate authority of the board of education, in practice many groups never come to the board's attention. Also, certain groups, such as district-level committees, may report directly to the curriculum director rather than reporting to individual building principals.

Because certain committees will create different lines of communication from the "ideal" illustrated in Figure 3-2, there will necessarily be a variety of authority patterns in use throughout the school and school system. For this reason, some pains must be taken to establish patterns of authority and to communicate them to the individuals involved.

It will be the supervisor's responsibility, therefore, first to develop a personal understanding of the degree of authority that he or she possesses and, second, to communicate that understanding to the work group. In this way, everyone concerned will know how each person fits into the overall pattern of authority.

To this end, some questions for the supervisor immediately come to mind, as indicated in Figure 3-4.

---

1. Who established the work group? To whom are the group's results to be communicated?

2. At what level of authority is the group authorized to work: information, recommendation, decision? Who granted that authority?

3. Who reports to me? To whom do I report?

FIGURE 3-4. Who's in Charge?

These fundamental questions should be asked not only by the group supervisor, but by every group member. The answers to these questions help to clarify how each person fits into the overall pattern of authority.

SUCCESSFUL JOB CHARTS

The answers to the basic questions in Figure 3-4 will lead to the creation of a job chart, which shows the total pattern of authority and responsibility for a specific "job," or goal. Figure 3-5 shows what one job chart might look like:

Team A	Team B	Team C
Ms. Swanson	Mrs. Smith	Mrs. Frank
Mr. Lawrence*	Ms. Judson	Mr. Perth
Mrs. Lloyd	Mr. Everett	Mrs. Larson*
Mr. Hart	Miss Johnson*	

ALL TEAMS REPORT TO THE
COORDINATING TEAM:

Mr. Lawrence, Miss Johnson, Mrs. Larson*

TOTAL TASK FORCE REVIEWS TEAM   Recommendation
FINDINGS.   Authority

Task Force Leader: Mrs. Larson

TASK FORCE REPORTS TO BUILDING Recommendation
PRINCIPAL FOR FURTHER REVIEW. Authority

Principal: Mr. Long

TASK FORCE RECOMMENDATION AND Decision
PRINCIPAL'S RECOMMENDATION ARE Authority
REPORTED TO THE CURRICULUM
DIRECTOR.

Curriculum Director: Mr. Frazier

---

*Coordinator/Leader

FIGURE 3-5. Gifted Committee Job Chart

This example—again following the elementary gifted program sample begun in Chapter Two—illustrates exactly who is in charge from subgroup level to final decision authority.

A successful job chart begins with the furthest breakdown of the work group—in this case, the three teams: A, B, and C. It then encompasses all individuals directly involved in the group activity *up to the decision authority.* Although other individuals may review group findings, their involvement after the decision has been made is peripheral to the job and, consequently, outside the scope of the job chart.

In the example in Figure 3-5, it must be assumed that the curric-

ulum director, Mr. Frazier, has the authority to approve and implement
—or disapprove—the gifted education program recommended by the
task force under the direction of Mrs. Larson. But note, also, that there
is a further stage of recommendation, that of the principal, Mr. Long.

In this job chart, the principal, who is called upon to review the
task force's recommendations, has these options:

1. He may pass the task force's recommendation on to the curric-
    ulum director with his own recommendation that the work be
    accepted or rejected.

2. He may urge the task force to rethink its recommendation if he
    disapproves of it. However, *the principal may not require the
    task force to suit its recommendation to his preference
    because he is not the decision authority.*

In this example, only the curriculum director, Mr. Frazier, has the
decision authority and only he has the responsibility of accepting or
rejecting the task force's recommendation and, equally, the recommendation of the principal, Mr. Long.

It is in this middle ground—the position of the principal, in this
instance—that problems tend to occur that can be prevented by conscientious use of a job chart. The principal's authority here does not
exceed that of the task force. Both possess *paralleled* authority. The
task force recommendation is reviewed by the principal for the purpose of providing information for his recommendation rather than for
the purpose of judging the merits of the recommendation.

In like manner, the curriculum director is really dealing with two
separate recommendations, not merely with one recommendation
that has passed through two stages.

A couple of variations suggest themselves:

1. The principal, Mr. Long, may be excluded from the task force
    process altogether. He may be provided with the task force's
    recommendation as a matter of information without being re-
    quired to make a separate recommendation of his own.

2. The principal and the curriculum director, Mr. Frazier, may
    share the decision authority. In this case, the job chart's final
    stages would look like this:

(Same initial stages as Figure 3-5.)

TASK FORCE REVIEWS TEAM FINDINGS. Task Force Leader: Mrs. Larson	Recommendation Authority
TASK FORCE RECOMMENDATION IS REPORTED TO MANAGEMENT TEAM. Team members: Mr. Long, Principal, and Mr. Frazier, Curriculum Director	Decision Authority

---

FIGURE 3-6. Shared Decision Authority

Whatever pattern of authority is chosen, it is important to the group's success that roles and responsibilities be well-defined and generally understood by all concerned. Creating and using job charts helps to create this clarity and understanding.

REINFORCING THE ROLE OF THE INDIVIDUAL

It is necessary to give some attention to group members' individual *levels of involvement*. In an earlier book,[1] I identified five levels of individual involvement. These levels are:

1. Information
2. Recommendation
3. Consultation
4. Authorization
5. Initiation

The levels are listed in increasing order of involvement. At the *information* level, ideas flow from the group leader to the individual member and/or vice versa.

At the *recommendation* level, individual group members may offer advice, suggestions, and recommendations to the leader.

At the *consultation* level, the leader seeks out such recommendations from the individuals prior to taking action on behalf of the group.

---

[1]Donovan R. Walling. *Complete Book of School Public Relations: An Administrator's Manual and Guide.* (Englewood Cliffs, New Jersey: Prentice-Hall, Inc., 1982). pp. 57–59.

At the *authorization* level, individual group members approve of actions to be taken by the group leader or by the group collectively.

Finally, at the *initiation* level, individual group members initiate new projects within the group.

Greater involvement on the part of individual group members tends generally to enhance feelings of ownership, and to generate more positive interaction between leaders and the group and, consequently, higher quality output.

As with the level of authority, the level of involvement of each individual will carry with it certain expectations that need to be considered. Many staff members will enjoy the added responsibility of functioning at the initiation level in a group situation. Other members may be less secure and may feel more comfortable working at lower levels of involvement.

Figure 3-7 shows an authority–involvement matrix that can be used to map the levels of involvement and authority of the various group members. It should be noted that the *authority* mapping is a constant—that is, group authority is established at the outset of group work. The *group's* level of authority does not change from individual to individual. On the other hand, *involvement* is an individual characteristic that will vary from one person to the next.

Mapping the individual group members may help the group leader to structure tasks and subgroups. In general, those individuals who fall nearest the lower left corner of the matrix will be most dependent on the leader, while those who fall toward the upper right corner of the matrix will be most autonomous.

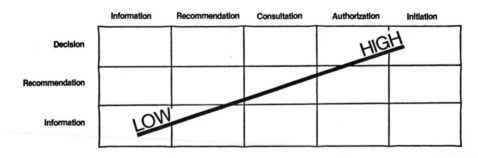

Authority – Involvement   Matrix

FIGURE 3-7

Each level of the matrix is valid for certain types of groups and for certain tasks and goals. Ideally, members of the group should feel comfortable at each level, depending upon the particular task at hand.

Understanding how authority and involvement interact will help the group leader to utilize each individual's strengths to the fullest extent and to minimize the impact of personal weaknesses on the total group effort.

RECOGNIZING AND REWARDING STAFF INVOLVEMENT

Not long ago, results of a survey by the Federal Labor Relations Institute indicated that the foremost factor in employee job satisfaction was "full appreciation of work done."[2] Other items on the survey included job security, working conditions, wages, and interesting work—all traditionally viewed by many supervisors as more important than appreciation. Nonetheless, employees seem to view recognition and reward as prime motivators.

(Interestingly enough, the second-ranked item turned out to be "feeling of being in on things," which effectively translates into involvement and ownership, qualities that will be stressed throughout this book.)

How, then, can staff involvement in school management be recognized and rewarded? Here are some suggestions:

1. Use Personal Letters of Appreciation

A sincere letter of commendation written directly to the individual is ample evidence of a job well done. The letter may be written by the group leader, or by a higher level supervisor, such as the superintendent or a board of education member. Letters of appreciation are more highly valued when a copy is also sent to the individual's direct supervisor (e.g., the building principal) and when a copy is filed with the staff member's personal records.

2. Use Public Recognition

While letters of appreciation are a fine form of private recognition, public acknowledgment is sometimes more valued. The letter of appreciation might be presented at a faculty meeting (at the building level or at the district level), or the individual might be given a certificate, a plaque, a pin, or some other token award. When service

---

[2]Will Lorey. "Everything You Need to Deliver Effective Delegation Training," *Training*, November 1981, pp. 38–43.

is newsworthy enough, a press release may be appropriate for community-wide recognition.

3. Use monetary rewards.

Business and industry often use monetary rewards, and there is no reason why such remuneration should not be considered in education as well. Staff involvement could easily earn points toward a monetary bonus. Other monetary-type rewards might center on priority equipment, donations to charities on behalf of certain schools or departments, and similar "rewards." Such monetary rewards do not necessarily have to come from district coffers, but may be contributed by parent groups, such as the local PTA chapter or the booster club. One point, however, should be stressed: *Money does not take the place of appreciation.* Work that is recognized and earns an appropriate "thank you" is important—with or without a monetary reward.

The keys to effective recognition and reward are these:

- *Sincerity*
  The recognition represents genuine appreciation for service rendered.
- *Personalization*
  Recognition suits the individual contribution.
- *Value*
  The reward is valued by the individual because it in some way contributes to his or her self-esteem.

More discussion of recognition and rewards is included in later chapters in conjunction with specific group situations.

FIVE POINTS TO REMEMBER

In viewing group and individual responsibility, here are five points worth remembering:

1. Understand *who* is responsible for *what* in any group context.
2. Recognize the importance of control and authority as integral elements of group work.
3. Develop appropriate ownership of group projects.

4. Design and maintain well-defined patterns of communication and job descriptions.

5. Recognize individual levels of involvement, and reward individual efforts and accomplishments.

These five guidelines will help to ensure that staff involvement is both satisfying to the participants and productive for the school or school district.

Gathering Staff Input Efficiently

4

BECAUSE few school work groups will need to gather information on a large scale, they will be more likely to need pinpoint information from selected sources. The techniques described in this chapter are designed to complement and help simplify this kind of focused information gathering.

SURVEYS—FISHING FOR FACTS

When I was growing up, my father used to say, "You won't find out unless you ask." I suspect that advice is given by many parents to their children. The same notion holds true for information gathering in the school work group setting. The information needed by the group won't just appear; it will have to be asked for.

Almost all information gathering centers on some form of survey. The word *survey* includes everything from open-ended questionnaires to checklists to telephone queries to so-called "opinionnaires." It's a potpourri term, a catch-all. What surveys amount to is fishing for facts. Like fishing, success will be achieved by using the right equipment, the right bait, and the right fishing hole. For surveys, those three "right things" translate to:

1. the right questions
2. the right people
3. the right time

FIVE QUALITIES OF EFFECTIVE SURVEYS

Good surveys have several points in common. These qualities may be summarized as follows:

1. An Effective Survey Targets Specific Questions

This quality is part of "the right questions." It means that the survey asks direct, pertinent questions. In developing the specific survey items, the survey writer(s) must always question:

"Is this what I (we) need to know?"

"Will this question yield the facts needed?"

Superfluous questions weaken the survey's efficiency, since they produce no information of merit and merely add to the tabulation process.

2. An Effective Survey Targets a Specific Audience

This is "the right people" quality. It means that the survey is administered to those individuals who have a stake in the questions. The survey respondents whose answers will yield the best information are those individuals to whom the questions are most pertinent.

The question the survey writer needs to ask is:

"Who can best answer these questions?"

3. An Effective Survey Is Timely

"The right time" for a survey is before problems become crises and before final decisions are made. It is often amazing to find a survey being taken to find out who doesn't like a particular decision *after the decision has been made.* What really is needed is a survey to find out preferences for decision options *before* the final decision is made.

Conflict is avoided and decisions are more valid when concerned individuals provide information—through a survey—that aids in the decision-making process rather than merely reviews a final decision after the fact.

Survey respondents function at the information level of authority. To do so effectively, they must be given the opportunity to provide timely input. An untimely survey can arouse anger (e.g., "Why wasn't I asked when it mattered?"), which is counterproductive to the group process and, ultimately, contributes to lowered morale.

4. An Effective Survey Should Be Short

Length is a factor in getting surveys answered in the first place. Short, pertinent surveys tend to yield more accurate results. They are also easier to tabulate and summarize.

Targeting surveys to appropriate audiences and topics will help narrow focus and keep surveys short.

5. An Effective Survey Is Easy to Answer

A good rule of thumb is that a survey should take only two to five minutes to answer. Keeping the survey short will help accomplish this goal, but form is another important consideration. Yes–no questions, checklists, and rating scales are easiest to answer. Twenty well-written questions can be completed in two or three minutes. And, the results will be easy to tabulate and report.

On the other hand, a narrative response can be valuable in certain instances. In these cases, a survey might be limited to three or four open-ended questions and still be easy to answer.

Where the survey is accurately targeted to a highly motivated, concerned audience, it will be possible to use longer surveys, which require greater time and concentration.

One way to tell whether the survey is on target is to look at the Not Applicable (N/A) responses. A high rate of Not Applicable responses will indicate that the survey is not reaching the concerns of the respondents or that it isn't reaching the right audience in the first place. Likewise, rate of return is another gauge of effectiveness. Surveys that are on target get answered; those that aren't, don't.

DESIGNING WRITTEN FORMS

Regardless whether the administration of the survey will be done in writing or orally, in person or by telephone, every survey should begin with a written form that serves as a guide and record.

Figures 4-1 to 4-4 show four forms:

Yes–No Questionnaire

Checklist Survey

Ranking Survey

Narrative Questionnaire

In order to compare and contrast the types of form design, the topic and potential audience for the surveys have been held constant in all four figures. Here's the situation:

A junior high school staff committee has been established to review the school's classroom tardiness policy. In order to find out how the total faculty feels about the issue of tardiness and to glean some ideas for revision from the staff, the committee decides to administer a survey. What follows is the survey in four potential forms.

Yes–No Questionnaire

Figure 4-1 shows a yes–no questionnaire on the topic of tardiness.

The main purpose of this form is to clarify how the staff feels about having a tardiness policy. Individual teachers may respond that

---

To the Faculty:
Please answer the following questions and return this form to Mrs. Larson by 4:00 P.M., Friday, October 8.

	Yes	No	Not Applicable
1. Is tardiness a problem in this school?	_____	_____	_____
2. Is tardiness a problem for you personally?	_____	_____	_____
3. Should the present tardiness policy be revised?	_____	_____	_____
4. Should there be a uniform tardiness policy?	_____	_____	_____
5. Should teachers be allowed flexibility in applying the policy?	_____	_____	_____

6. Describe the tardiness policy you favor (if not the one currently used). _____

_____

_____

_____

FIGURE 4-1. Tardiness Policy Questionnaire

tardiness is not a problem, or that it seems to be a problem for others but not for them personally. They may feel that the present policy is adequate, or that there shouldn't be a uniform policy at all. They may or may not indicate a desire for flexibility in application. These are the essential yes–no questions.

Because the committee is also looking for suggestions that cannot be gained in the yes–no process, one open-ended question is also included. Notice, too, the inclusion of the Not Applicable answer column. Since not all staff members are teachers, some questions may not apply to them. A good example is the librarian, who may have some stake in whether or not there is an enforceable tardiness policy, but for whom the classroom questions are inappropriate. Certain specialists could also fit into this category.

Checklist Survey

Similar information may be gathered using a checklist, as shown in Figure 4-2.

To the Faculty:
Please complete the following checklist by checking those statement with which you *agree.* Return this form to Mrs. Larson by 4:00 P.M., Friday, October 8.

I Agree:

_____ Tardiness is a problem in this school.

_____ Tardiness is a problem for me personally.

_____ The present tardiness policy should be revised.

_____ There should be a uniform tardiness policy.

_____ Teachers should be allowed flexibility in applying a tardiness policy.

If you believe the present tardiness policy should be revised, describe the policy you favor. _____

_____

_____

_____

FIGURE 4-2. Tardiness Policy Checklist

The checklist is rather like the yes–no questionnaire without the double answer option. Instead, the respondent simply checks those statements with which he or she agrees.

The advantage of the checklist is that it is slightly quicker to answer than the yes–no questionnaire and may appeal, therefore, to less concerned respondents. These individuals will see that it is an easy, uncomplicated form and answer it even though they may feel that they have no particular stake in the results.

Conversely, the checklist's disadvantage is that tabulators will have no way of knowing whether non-checked items are disagreed with or whether they are simply not applicable to that respondent.

Notice, too, that the single open-ended question has been retained in order to gain ideas for the new policy should such a need emerge.

Ranking Survey

Figure 4-3 shows how the items in the previous two forms might be arranged for a ranking survey.

To the Faculty:
Please rank the following statements from 1 to 5. (1 = least important; 5 = most important) Return this form to Mrs. Larson by 4:00 P.M., Friday, October 8.

Rank

Tardiness is a problem in this school.   _____

Tardiness is a problem for me personally.   _____

The present tardiness policy should be revised.   _____

There should be a uniform tardiness policy.   _____

Teachers should be allowed flexibility in applying a tar-
diness policy.   _____

If you believe the present tardiness policy should be revised, please describe the policy you favor.

_____

_____

_____

FIGURE 4-3. Tardiness Policy Ranking

Ranking is asking the staff to determine their collective priorities. Which is more important to the total faculty: the tardiness problem itself or the desire for flexibility in applying a tardiness policy?

Using the ranking form of survey can help the committee to determine better the direction that their efforts should take in order to meet the staff's needs. As in previous examples, the open-ended question will allow individuals who do want the policy revised to state the kinds of changes they desire.

Narrative Questionnaire

Figure 4-4 takes the material used in the previous figures and structures it completely in open-ended fashion, thereby eliciting a narrative response on the part of each survey participant.

The narrative questionnaire, in addition to gathering basic information, allows staff members to vent their frustrations and concerns in their own unique manner. In some instances, the narrative responses can be more enlightening than shorter responses.

To the Faculty:

Please respond to the following questions and return this form to Mrs. Larson by 4:00 P.M., Friday, October 8.

Is tardiness a problem for you personally or do you view it as a whole-school problem? Explain.

_____

_____

Should there be a uniform tardiness policy? If so, should it be different from the policy we have now? How? _____

_____

_____

If a uniform policy is adopted, what degree of flexibility should individual teachers be allowed in applying the policy? _____

_____

_____

FIGURE 4-4. Tardiness Policy Questionnaire

At the same time, narrative questionnaires are often viewed negatively as too time-consuming or—when the subject is particularly
sensitive—too revealing, even though the form does not ask the individual to identify him- or herself. This raises the question: Is anonymity acceptable?

For most situations, there is no reason to know exactly who fills
out which form. Surveys gather data in the "long view" and are not intended to serve as personal opinion vehicles. At the same time, there
may be occasions when knowing the respondent's identity could prove
useful—e.g., when the committee is willing to provide individual
answers to specific respondent questions, thus using the survey in a
dual role as information gatherer and internal public relations tool.
When this is the case, an optional line asking for the respondent's
name and, possibly, manner of being reached (address, telephone
number, room number, etc.) can easily be incorporated into the final
form.

ENSURING A TIMELY RETURN

Part of ensuring a timely return comes with assuring that the
survey is returned at all. This assurance is firmest when the five qualities described earlier are embodied in the survey. In building the four
example questionnaires (Figures 4-1 to 4-4), these qualities have been
faithfully represented:

- the surveys are directed to a specific audience, the school staff
  that will be working with the tardiness policy under consideration;
- the surveys use specific questions about the advisability of having a tardiness policy and how it should be used, as well as
  gather suggestions for potential revision;
- the surveys (presumably) are administered in the early stages of
  committee consideration, so that the results can be used to
  direct appropriate emphasis;
- the surveys are short, using only five points in most instances;
  and
- the surveys are easy to answer because the directions and the
  questions are clearly and simply stated.

Another element of timeliness is setting a deadline. Notice that
this has been done in each of the examples. Each form contains the

line, "Return this form to Mrs. Larson by 4:00 P.M., Friday, October 8." It is important to include not only *when* the form is to be returned, but *who* is to receive it. If you're like me, you've received countless intraschool forms giving a deadline of when they are to be turned in only to be left wondering who to give them to. Avoid this pitfall if you expect a timely return.

Similarly, it is assumed in the examples that all staff members know who Mrs. Larson is and where she can be located in order to turn in the survey once it's completed. If Mrs. Larson, or whoever, is not universally known, it will be essential to fill in the missing information. For example:

"Return this form to Mrs. Larson, *Room 202, Foxworth Elementary School*, by 4:00 P.M., Friday, October 8."

A timely return is more likely to result from a timely distribution. A good rule of thumb is to allow no more than a week for respondents to fill out and return the form. Less time is often preferable, especially with very short surveys, because people will tend to put off answering the questions until close to the deadline. The earlier the form is distributed, the greater the risk that it will be mislaid or forgotten.

Finally, a timely return can be ensured readily by *personally* administering the survey—that is, by orally asking the questions and recording the respondents' answers. Consumer surveys are often administered this way. (Remember those folks with the clipboards in the shopping mall?) There is no reason this method can't work in education as well. All it takes is a sufficient number of volunteers to ask the questions. Staff members can be approached in the lunchroom, teacher workroom, or lounge, as they check in in the morning, or at other convenient times and places.

Checklists and yes–no questionnaires—even fairly long ones—can be effectively administered using the personal approach, and the results may be more complete than pencil-and-paper administrations. However, personal administration does not allow for an anonymity factor and, thus, sensitive subjects cannot be handled easily in this fashion. Also, the personal administration method is cumbersome for ranking surveys and, unless both questions and answers are short, can be next to impossible for narrative questionnaires. Nonetheless, personal administration is an option worth considering for the appropriate circumstance.

USING THE TELEPHONE APPROACH

Another way of personally administering the survey is to use the telephone. Sometimes, it may be advantageous to take the survey out of the school setting. Telephoning staff members at home in the evening is a possible solution.

Here are some guidelines for successful telephone surveys:

1. Use a short survey—yes–no questionnaires and checklist surveys work best.
2. Have a separate form for each call, rather than trying to tabulate several calls on a single form.
3. Use a telephone script (see Figure 4-5) to avoid chitchat and improve efficiency.
4. Keep each call short and stick to business. On an average, survey calls should last no more than five minutes.
5. Call at an appropriate time. The best time to reach most teachers at home is between six and seven o'clock in the evening.
6. Thank the respondents for the information they have provided and let them know if a copy of the survey results will be available at a later time.

Keeping these guidelines in mind, Figure 4-5 demonstrates how one of the previous survey samples might be handled over the telephone.

By keeping the script short, polite, and businesslike, the survey administrator is able to get the information needed in a minimum amount of time. Notice that the respondent has been referred to by name several times. This helps to personalize the call, giving the respondent a sense of ownership in the information and how it will be used.

For sensitive subjects, the telephone survey—much like the personally administered survey—leaves little room for anonymity. However, some anonymity can be provided by including in the script a line such as: "We are gathering general information with this survey and none of the individuals who respond to the questions will be named in the final report." This statement helps to assure the respondent that his or her identity will go no farther than the questioner.

Notice, too, that if the telephone respondent is not available to talk at the time of the call, you should attempt to ascertain a better call-

DIAL NUMBER AND GET A RESPONSE

"Hello, _____. This is Jane Larson from Foxworth Elementary School. The Tardiness Policy Committee is taking a survey to determine how faculty members feel about the present tardiness policy and whether it ought to be revised. May I take about three minutes of your time to see how you feel about these questions?

NEGATIVE RESPONSE:

"May I call you back at _____?"

GET A RESPONSE.

"Thanks, _____
I'll call you back at

_____.

Goodbye."

POSITIVE RESPONSE:

"Thanks for your willingness to help out, _____.
Just answer these questions with 'yes' or 'no.' "

ADMINISTER THE SURVEY.

"Number One: Is tardiness a problem in your/our school?"

GET A RESPONSE.

"Number Two: Is tardiness a problem for you personally?"

GET A RESPONSE . . . AND SO ON.

WHEN THE QUESTIONS HAVE BEEN ANSWERED.

If the respondent favors a policy change, ask:
"Would you describe the tardiness policy you favor?"
Note response—do not discuss it. Go to closing.

If the respondent favors no change, go to closing.

"Thank you again for helping out with the survey, _____
The committee plans to tabulate the results and announce them at the faculty meeting next week. Goodbye."

FIGURE 4-5. Telephone Survey Script

ing time. If a better time is set, affirm that time by restating it. Then keep the commitment to call back.

Brief scripting of this sort ensures that the survey call does not become a gripe session or disintegrate into time-wasting gossip. By sticking firmly with the script, no vital information is omitted and the caller accomplishes more by managing time efficiently.

Telephone surveys are a good way to take the survey out of the school setting, away from the pressures of the workday. And, the personal contact of the telephone helps to ensure a higher response rate, while at the same time performing a positive internal public relations function.

PLANNING FOR "AUTOMATIC" TABULATION

Even the shortest, simplest surveys can turn into headaches when it comes time to tabulate the results. In most cases, someone (or perhaps several individuals) are delegated to sit down with pencil and paper and record the individual responses. The most common way this is done uses the age-old system of hash marks:

Yes   卌 || No ///

However, this system is time consuming and can become inaccurate for large numbers of responses simply because of the tedium involved.

A little advance planning will avoid these traditional pitfalls of hand-tabulated surveys.

Design the survey to fit onto a single sheet of paper. Keep the questions running across the full sheet, rather than making double columns. If more than one side of paper is needed, use a second sheet instead of using the back of the sheet.

In producing multiple copies of the survey, make certain that all forms are registered the same—i.e., so that the information on any one form lines up with the information on all the other forms.

After the surveys are filled in, instead of tabulating with the hash-mark method, simply cut each question and answer away from the sheet. Stack the finished forms together and use a paper cutter to separate the questions several sheets at a time.

Once there are piles of question strips, all the tabulators need to do is separate each pile into yes–no, checked–not checked, or rank number subpiles. Counting the number of responses in the subpiles is quicker than counting hash marks and often more accurate because the piles can be easily recounted if a question arises. When questions come up in the hash-mark method, the entire set of surveys has to be retabulated.

Registering the printed forms is not difficult, since for most surveys only a single master copy is used. Whether the forms are produced by spirit duplicator, mimeograph, or professional offset, there is usually no difficulty in producing a body of identical forms. The key, of course, is in the design of the master.

This *cut-and-count method* works for long or short surveys. Unless sophisticated machine-scoring and/or computer tabulation is readily available (including an expert to assist in the operation), the cut-and-count technique is probably the easiest and most efficient method of "automatic" tabulation available.

COMMON SENSE AND SUCCESSFUL SURVEYS

In the final analysis, the best guide to successful surveys is ordinary common sense.

Asking the question, "How would I answer this survey?" is an excellent way for the survey designer to approach the information-gathering task. It helps to keep the survey tactic from becoming mechanistic.

And, keep in mind the five qualities described at the beginning of this chapter:

Ask specific questions

Target a specific audience

Keep the survey timely

Make sure the form is short

Keep the questions easy-to-answer

Good surveys boil down to asking the right people the right questions at the right time.

The next chapter describes what to do with the information after it has been gathered.

How to Simplify and Systematize Your Recordkeeping and Reporting

5

THE emphasis in *How to Build Staff Involvement in School Management* has been on gathering information from staff, either through the work group or through some form of survey, as explored in Chapter Four. Naturally, committees and task forces may find that they need to gather information in other ways as well. These ways may include traditional historical research or the maintenance of anecdotal records.

Collecting historical research—examining legal statutes, district policies, contracts, and so on—involves traditional research methods with which educators are generally familiar.

Yet another form of recordkeeping is the maintenance of anecdotal records. This form of ongoing information gathering is discussed later on, since it relies more on consistency than on any particularly innovative "method."

Different forms of information gathering will be used to meet a variety of goals in many different situations by school work groups. The purpose of this chapter is to explore how information gathered through all forms of research can be simplified and systematized for more efficient use in the group work forum.

COMPILING INFORMATION—A SEGREGATED CARD FILE

No manual information filing system can compete with the rapid efficiency of a modern computer, but it is possible to use some of the computer-processing logic in simple, manual ways to assist in developing good recordkeeping.

The key to rapid information retrieval is *categorizing*. By breaking data into distinct categories, it is possible to call up specific bits of information without having to sort through the entire file. A variety of terms in computer jargon are applied to this idea of categories. An example in education that comes immediately to mind is the ERIC (Educational Resources Information Center) system. ERIC uses categorical labels, called *descriptors*, to computer file and locate information gleaned from education journals, abstracts, dissertations, and other sources that are often unavailable to the general reader. By using the correct descriptor or combination of descriptors, the ERIC user can locate information in the desired topic area.

In a manual form, the segregated card file works on the same principle. As researched information is gathered, it is sorted into categories. Each category is given a descriptive label. Some examples are shown in Figure 5-1, using the example of the committee that was charged with reviewing the school tardiness policy.

As you can see, the categorical labels include a main term, such as "SURVEY RESULTS," and then a subterm that further segregates the information. In this way, a group worker looking for what teachers

---

LEGAL STATUTES, Absenteeism and Tardiness
POLICY, Board of Education
POLICY, Evans Elementary
POLICY, Foxworth Elementary
RECOMMENDATIONS, Foxworth Parents
RECOMMENDATIONS, Foxworth Students
RECOMMENDATIONS, Foxworth Teachers
SURVEY RESULTS, Foxworth Parents
SURVEY RESULTS, Foxworth Students
SURVEY RESULTS, Foxworth Teachers

FIGURE 5-1. Descriptive Labels for Tardiness Data

said in response to the survey would not have to sort through the other parent and student survey results as well. The segregated card file makes it possible to retrieve information quickly and easily.

Another suggestion that sometimes proves helpful is color coding the various categories. This has the effect of visually separating different pieces of information so that they can be located more readily. Colored index cards can be purchased at most office supply outlets.

Many times, the information gathered by a school work group can be kept on 3″ × 5″ or 5″ × 7″ index cards. Either size is equally suitable, depending on the amount of space needed. But what if neither size offers enough space?

The answer is to apply the categorizing system to standard file folders. Where the card system is adequate for most group work purposes, the folders have the advantage of being able to hold bulky materials, such as letters from parents, newspaper clippings, actual copies of legal statutes, board of education policy handouts, and so on.

Use the folders or the index cards effectively by choosing *logical, specific category labels* to describe collected information.

Naturally, both card and folder filing systems should be alphabetized and, if necessary, cross-referenced. An example of cross-referencing is:

```
BOARD OF EDUCATION POLICY
   See POLICY, Board of Education
```

Another is:

```
SURVEY RECOMMENDATIONS
   See RECOMMENDATION (by group)
```

Where two or more descriptive categories might seem appropriate, the best one should be chosen as the label to be used and the others should be listed and cross-referenced to the main label.

As a card file grows, it may be advantageous to develop a separate index of the labels used in the file. This index sheet can be kept in the front of the file drawer or taped to the side of the file cabinet, or otherwise located near the file. Even though the file itself is alphabetized and easy to use, an index may help locate information faster in the case of large information collections.

The segregated card file has yet another advantage. As microcomputers become more available to schools across the nation, groups whose information is maintained on a continuous basis may want to convert to computer data storage. The categorical filing system described here is ready-made for such conversion with little or no need for adaptation.

DEVELOPING CLEAR TABLES OF FACTS

All of us have sat through meetings in which a large amount of information was given orally. Unless we were intimately familiar with the data presented, we probably ended up wondering what the presenter was talking about. The presenter failed to realize that an important part of any presentation is showing as well as telling.

As educators, we know that in order to get information across to our audience we need to show what we're talking about. Can you imagine teaching an art class without ever showing your students a drawing or a painting? The cliché "a picture is worth a thousand words" is never more true than in presenting factual information clearly.

Much of the information that is gathered by school work groups eventually must be presented, either to the group collectively or to an audience outside the work group. In most cases, data are summarized in some form of table. Therefore, it is appropriate to give some attention to developing tables of facts for presentation and recordkeeping.

Here are several guidelines to bear in mind.

1. *Limit the information included in each table or chart.* It is easier for readers/viewers to grasp a few facts at a time rather than comprehend "the whole ball of wax" at once.

2. *Limit the scope of the information in each table.* Similarly, audience members will grasp presented information better if it is limited in terms of time and spatial dimensions. For instance, a table limited to five years' worth of data would probably be clearer than one covering twenty years. In other words, limit not only the *amount* of data but also the *intensity* of the data.

3. *Segregate information categorically.* Do not mix dissimilar kinds of information. Jumbled information is likely to lead to equally jumbled comprehension.

4. *Sequence information appropriately.* When several tables or charts are used, place them so that one set of facts logically leads to the next. The audience should be able to see the relationship that exists among the various pieces of information.

5. *Use visual keys to highlight information effectively.* In addition to presenting words and numbers in tables, emphasize important points by using underlining, boldface type, italics, or colors. These alternatives to standard typing or printing help draw attention to those facts that should be noticed or remembered.

Keeping these guidelines in mind when preparing written reports or presentations helps to ensure that important material is noticed and understood.

ILLUSTRATING DATA EFFECTIVELY

It will often be helpful to present data in the form of illustrations rather than—or in addition to—presenting them as tables.

Two popular, easy-to-use types of illustrations are bar graphs and pie charts.

Bar Graphs

A bar graph illustrates the relationship among two or more facts of the same nature.

For example, a bar graph might be used to show a school's enrollment in one year as compared to one or more previous years—or even as compared to future enrollment projections. Similarly, a bar graph might compare the enrollments of several schools in the same year.

Figure 5-2 shows the three basic forms for bar graphs.

In general, horizontal and vertical bar graphs exhibit little difference between them; the choice of one or the other will depend on the nature of the data to be displayed. The floating bar graph differs from these other two in that it shows variable starting points. Both the horizontal and vertical forms assume an identical starting point for all compared facts. When beginning as well as end points in a comparison differ, the floating bar graph is able to show these differences. An example of this distinction is found in Figure 5-3.

It is often a good idea to make some visual distinction between the various bars in a graph. Unless sophisticated color printing methods are used to make these visual distinctions, it will be easiest to use lines, grids, and dots to "texture" the individual bars visually.

The textures shown in Figure 5-3 come in sheet form (called *shading film*) and are inexpensive and available at most office supply and graphic arts supply stores. Printed on transparent material that is self-adhesive, the texture is applied to the graph and the excess simply is cut away. (Another form of visual texture is similar to press-off letter-ing; it is also easy to use and readily available.)

Visual distinctions make the graphs easier to understand and more impressive-looking than plain illustrations. The investment of a small amount of time and effort pays off in clearer information presentations.

Note, too, that the guidelines set forth earlier have been adhered to in the visual illustration in Figure 5-3:

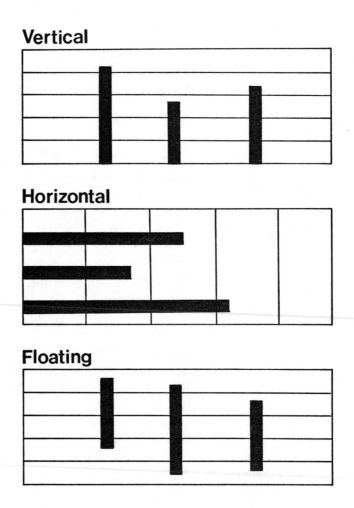

Vertical

Horizontal

Floating

FIGURE 5-2

Limited amount of information

Limited scope of information

Categorically distinct

Appropriately sequenced

Visually highlighted

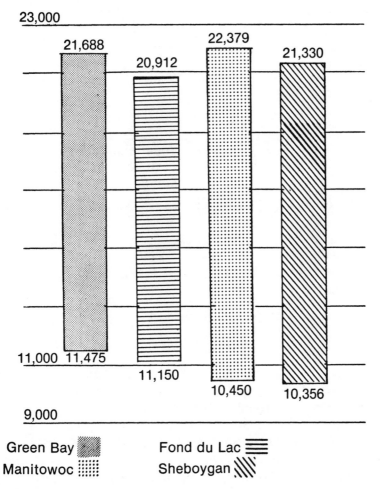

Minimum-Maximum Salary Offered in Athletic Conference (excluding longevity)

Green Bay
Manitowoc

Fond du Lac
Sheboygan

Salaries computed on school year: 57% Jan. to June
43% Sep. to Dec.

FIGURE 5-3

Pie Charts

A pie chart illustrates the relationship of parts to a whole.

The two things most often illustrated by pie charts are time and money. For example, a pie chart might show how the principal spends his or her day, the racial or economic breakdown of a school or school district, or how the school budget is spent.

Figure 5-4 shows how the graduates of one high school plan to spend the year after graduation.

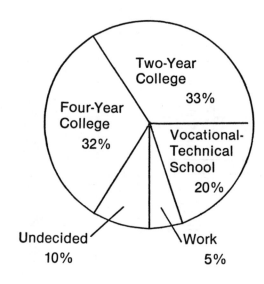

FIGURE 5-4

This type of pie graph might well be the product of a curriculum study committee looking at how the school's program of studies fits the future educational needs of its students.

Often, pie charts for monetary figures are represented pictorially as coins, such as shown in Figure 5-5. Such visual representations are good ways to call attention to the facts in an interesting manner. Keeping the reader interested in the facts helps to assure that the information is both read and digested.

And, of course, a pie chart doesn't have to be round. Taking the image of a dollar bill, for example, and visually dividing it into the

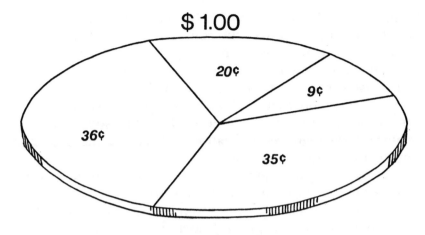

FIGURE 5-5

categorical amounts represented in a departmental budget may be just as effective as the more traditional round pie chart.

In addition to bar graphs and pie charts, other forms of data illustrations may occasionally be called for in both written reports and/or oral presentations. The key to illustrating tabular kinds of information effectively lies in striving for these three goals:

1. Clarity

Illustrations should make data more understandable to the reader/viewer. They should take complex sets of facts and simplify them by limiting the amount and scope of information shown at one time.

2. Order

Illustrations should demonstrate orderliness through the use of appropriate categorization and sequencing of information.

3. Interest

Illustrations should create interest on the part of the viewer/reader because they present an alternative to and accompaniment for the written report form.

More about using visuals in oral presentations is included in Chapter Six.

MAINTAINING ONGOING INFORMATION COLLECTION

Implicit in the structure of and charge to some school work groups is the need for a continuing effort at information collection. In some instances, this means that the group will design a series of surveys to be administered over the course of several weeks, months, or even years. Or the group may design a survey to be given repetitively, such as an annual teacher attitude questionnaire.

In these cases, the procedure for maintaining records does not differ materially from that outlined earlier in this chapter. The only addition to the system described before should be some form of dating procedure to distinguish information gathered at one time from similar information gathered at another time.

In considering ongoing information collection, it is appropriate to look at another form, anecdotal records.

Anecdotal information comes from many sources: telephone calls to group members or the group leader/coordinator; casual conversations with staff members, parents, or students; contacts outside the school with community members; letters; newspaper articles; and so on. This input is diverse and unsystematic. The key to using anecdotal information effectively is to bring order out of the chaos—*to build anecdotal records systematically.*

Here are some suggestions I offered in a previous work dealing with anecdotal information[1]:

- Create a telephone log. Write down the caller's name, the date and the time of the call, and, briefly, the substance of the conversation.

- Develop a file of pertinent newspaper articles, ads, letters to the editor, editorials, etc., that bear on the group work. Don't forget to include student and staff newspapers and newsletters.

- Write brief summaries of radio and television programs that provide information on the group topic. Public broadcasting and local community forum programming are ripe for anecdotal information gathering.

- Note casual contacts in diary fashion in much the same way as telephone calls are logged.

- Collect letters, pamphlets, other groups' surveys, and other printed material that contributes useful information.

As material comes in, it can be filed in the same way that more formally gathered information is maintained.

---

[1]Donovan R. Walling, *Complete Book of School Public Relations: An Administrator's Manual and Guide* (Englewood Cliffs, NJ: Prentice-Hall, Inc., 1982), pp. 35–36.

By utilizing all information sources—whether they be gathered through staff surveys, historical research, or anecdotal contacts—school work groups will be able to build complete informational bases from which to proceed toward the group goal in the most efficient manner possible.

BREAKING THE "BIG JOB" INTO WORKABLE BITS

A fundamental principle of effective organization that has been consistently reiterated in this book is the notion of breaking the "big job" into workable bits. The principle applies when committees and task forces are divided into subgroups as well as when gathered information is categorized and filed under main and subordinate headings.

Part of the effectiveness of information gathering, recordkeeping, and reporting depends on the ability of group leaders and members to delegate appropriate tasks effectively.

It is particularly in this area of what might be called "human data processing" that concerned individuals are most likely to take on more than they can reasonably manage. When this happens, not only does the individual suffer under the strain of overwork, but the group suffers from a breakdown of efficiency.

There are many plausible reasons for not delegating, ranging from the traditional "If you want a job done right, do it yourself" to the leader's lament of "How can I keep abreast of the group if I don't do the job myself?" While these excuses seem reasonable on the surface, some clear thinking will reveal that there are probably several other individuals who will do just as good a job, or better, and that there are other ways of keeping up-to-date without doing everything personally.

Delegating applies not only to the group leader but to the members, because delegation can be accomplished both upward and downward in the organizational hierarchy. It can also be accomplished laterally among the various group members. Important to the collection- storage-retrieval-report process is finding the right person for the right job.

- Who is adept at filing?
- Who handles figures and statistics easily?
- Who knows the background behind the data?
- Who is handy with illustrations?

In other words, job charts and a discussion about individual roles (Chapter Three) must extend logically into the recordkeeping/reporting of any school work group. Fitting the particular skills of individual group members into the overall scheme of the group's work is elemental in assuring that the group functions successfully. This means that every group's main goal should be treated as a big job and should be broken into workable bits to utilize everyone's strengths to the fullest degree possible.

A FEW WORDS OF CAUTION

Someone once said: "Manage information, don't let it manage you." It's good advice for the recordkeeper. With this idea in mind, here are some cautions.

1. Collect information that is truly needed.

No survey should go out nor should any historical research be pursued until the question "Do we really need this information?" has been answered. No piece of data should be gathered unless it is established that the information will be used in the group's work. This is not to say that certain types of information cannot be collected *on speculation*, but such speculation should be well-founded.

2. Discard unneeded and outdated information.

Information collected on speculation that does not prove useful should be discarded. Likewise, data that are obsolete should be gotten rid of. Files that are full of useless information are inefficient, take up space, slow down information retrieval, and may inadvertently mislead researchers. Get rid of them!

3. Be aware of sensitive information.

Competent legal authority should be consulted before collecting sensitive information in areas such as race, religion, sex, sexual preferences, national origin, and age. Similarly, both the gathering of and subsequent access to information such as personnel records, medical and/or psychological records, and student records should be studied seriously prior to activity in these and similar areas.

FOUR GUIDES TO GOOD RECORDKEEPING AND REPORTING

Four summary points to keep in mind when designing a recordkeeping system are:

1. Build a system that is simple to maintain but that also allows for the expansion of information, both in the amount of data kept and in the complexity of that data.

2. Develop information in tables and illustrations that clarify and emphasize appropriately in order to enhance levels of understanding.

3. Delegate information gathering and recordkeeping so that individual group members' skills are used to their fullest extent.

4. Guard against the potential abuse of information through the misuse of sensitive data and the use of obsolete information.

The fundamentals of recordkeeping and reporting discussed in this chapter will remain applicable as more and more schools move into the computer age. Already, many schools possess their own microcomputers. Not long ago the use of computers in school management was limited to class scheduling and grade reporting, and even these tasks were usually contracted out to specialized educational computer services. Today, many school offices use their own microcomputers to build master schedules, keep track of student attendance, and perform other routine chores.

Many of the recordkeeping and statistical analysis tasks described in this chapter are becoming available on computer software. As office personnel, administrators, and teachers become more proficient in microcomputer operation, these software programs can be put into service for more efficient recordkeeping and reporting.

It is not a very daring prediction to foresee the growing use of in-house computers for additional management tasks, such as handling the information storage for various staff work groups. Computers have the capacity to do everything from storing addresses to writing short stories,[2] and educators are daily learning more about how to use them. By building a foundation of systematic recordkeeping practices, it will be possible to take advantage of technological progress in data processing as it becomes available to schools.

---

[2]For a glimpse of the future and a look at a short story writing computer, read R. C. Newell's article, "Thus Wrote Racter" in the Spring 1982 issue of the AFT journal, *American Educator.*

Building Personal Presentation Skills

6

ALMOST everyone finds him- or herself in leadership or spokesperson roles at one time or another. It may be as the coordinator of a sub-group or the leader of a larger group. Regardless of what form the group assumes, how that group functions and how its ideas and conclusions are presented to others will depend to a significant degree on the personal abilities of the group's leader and spokesperson.

FEELING COMFORTABLE IN YOUR ROLE

One of the worst fears of many people is that of speaking before an audience. Whether the audience is large or small is inconsequential. Surprisingly, educators are not exempt from this phobia, despite years of practice in speaking before classrooms full of students in most instances. There's just something different about talking to adults.

To assert that these fears are largely groundless and imaginary, while true, is of no particular value. What is needed is a way to feel more comfortable in the presentation role, which is a combination of roles that may be identified as follows:

Director: Establishes group directions, tasks, etc. Makes work assignments, basic decisions.

Coordinator: Synthesizes disparate conclusions. Develops schedules, timelines, flow charts, etc.

Facilitator: Provides for group forums, idea exchanges. Secures support: facilities, materials, expert assistance.

Contact: Fields inquiries from other staff and the public. Responds to media representatives.

Reporter: Presents group conclusions in written and/or oral form to external individuals and groups—i.e., the superintendent, the board of education, and so on.

The five roles may be grouped further into the traditional categories of leader and spokesperson:

A leader is . . .	*A spokesperson is . . .*
a director	a contact
a coordinator	a reporter
a facilitator	

Both leader and spokespersons fall under the umbrella of the presentation role. Understanding these various individual roles, however, is the first step in feeling more comfortable with the larger responsibility.

Security comes from knowing what you are supposed to do. Every time a new employee begins work, he or she feels uncertain. New situations cause anxiety to the employee because they present no clear definition of what the individual is supposed to do. As the new job begins to unfold, the individual finds out what his or her role is and begins to function effectively and to feel secure in the new situation.

Understanding the presentation role you are to play, therefore, will bring security and understanding which will enable you to be more effective in the new role. The stumbling block in most cases is that initial learning period—that time when the individual is "finding out" what to do. This time period can be shortened and, consequently, efficiency can be improved by better defining the role of presentation. Or, if you are that individual, you will feel more comfortable sooner by taking time to examine your own role as a beginning step toward effectively functioning in that role.

ALTERNATIVE MODES OF GROUP LEADERSHIP

In traditional parlance, leadership modes run the gamut from autocratic to laissez-faire. The dictator or autocratic leader must control everything. He or she is *the* decision maker who directs, coordinates, and facilitates with an iron hand. The laissez-faire leader, on the other hand, is laid back. He or she doesn't control or direct. Things just seem to happen and this leader "goes with the flow."

Most leaders actually fall somewhere in between these two extremes. Where the individual fits on the continuum is a question for personal speculation. More important, perhaps, is to take a different viewpoint regarding the continuum itself. This alternative viewpoint is what I call *creative leadership*.

Creative leadership is a personal outlook that serves to modify how leaders perceive their tasks and interact with those individuals and groups for whom they are responsible.

Here's how creative leadership works.

If someone gave you a box of odd bicycle parts and said "Make something," what would you create? (Besides a bicycle, of course.)

One response, for example, might be to fashion a piece of sculpture, using just the handlebars and the saddle. That's what Pablo Picasso did to create his famous sculpture, "Bull's Head," in 1943.

To Picasso, the shape of the bicycle saddle turned on end suggested a bull's face. The bicycle handlebars, set above the saddle, looked like horns.

As with the creativity shown by Picasso, creative leadership is the ability to respond to new viewpoints to produce ideas—and encourage others to produce ideas—that are unusual and original, and to elaborate on those ideas.

Creative leadership stems from personal creativity, which is essentially a learned attitude characterized by a willingness to explore uncharted ground. It certainly is not limited to the arts. There are creative answers to most questions—the trick is to be open to finding them.

Some personal goals for the creative leader might be:

1. Set an Individual Standard and Encourage Others to Do So

Competition can produce rivalry between individuals and between groups that can be destructive to morale and accomplishment. Competition with oneself is healthier and more productive.

One way to firm up personal standards is to write them down. There's something about seeing a personal goal in black and white that strengthens an individual's resolve. Set group goals the same way: Write them down and post them in a conspicuous place.

2. Aim for Success but Be Realistic

Set individual and group goals and tasks that are challenging but within the grasp of the individual or group. On a personal level, for instance, if you've never built a television set or worked much in electronics, it is probably not reasonable to set a goal of building your own stereo system—at least, not at first. It would be more realistic to try your hand with a simple radio kit to begin with, and then work up to more complex projects.

In other words, aim for success, not for frustration and disappointment. Breaking the "Big Job" into workable bits, grouping and subgrouping, and scheduling enough time and resources to do the job are some of the considerations that account for successful work groups.

3. Emphasize Positive Thinking

Set a personal example for others in the work group. The road to failure is paved with negative thoughts. While a certain amount of grumbling and complaining is normal in any group situation, constant bickering and negative expressions betray a dangerous undercurrent. Endeavor to discover what the problems are and treat the cause of the negativity.

"We did it before."

"It's too radical."

"The faculty won't go for it."

"That's not in the budget."

"We've never done it before."

"Let's table it for now."

"Our school is different."

"The school board won't like it."

"We've always done it this way."

"Not enough time this year."

"It's impossible."

FIGURE 6-1. Idea Killers, or "It's a Good Idea, But . . ."

Also, encourage positive discussions. Provide for nonjudgmental brainstorming and other ways of airing group members' ideas. Avoid the "It's a good idea, but . . ." syndrome that kills creative thinking. Figure 6-1 lists just a few of the idea killers to be aware of and eliminate from group discussions.

4. Seek and Encourage Varied Approaches to Problem Solving

Part of creative leadership is openness to variety and new ideas. New ways of doing things merit experimentation. The ability and willingness to become aware of different outlooks and to test new hypotheses will lead to innovative discoveries.

Try this experiment sometime. Next time you see a colleague glance at his or her watch, ask that person what time it is. Nine out of ten people will have to look at their watch a second time in order to tell you. Why? Because most people don't really look to see what time it is. They look to see if it is the time they *thought* it was.

In other words, these people aren't discovering anything. Instead, they are confirming or verifying a preconception.

The creative leader is one who looks for the real discovery. Discard preconceptions and seek out the new.

Whether the individual in the leadership role—the director-coordinator-facilitator—leans more toward the autocratic or the laissez-faire end of the leadership continuum, the adoption of a creative leadership stance will enhance the efficiency of the group with which the leader works.

Now, what about the other part of the presentation role, that of spokesperson?

ORGANIZING TO BECOME A SUCCESSFUL SPOKESPERSON

There is a quotation by Lao-Tzu, the founder of Taoism, that aptly frames the qualities necessary to be a successful spokesperson:

> Become unaffected;
> Cherish sincerity;
> Belittle the personal;
> Reduce desires.

These sentiments can be stated in the following way for developing success as a spokesperson:

1. Learn to Speak Directly About the Topic at Hand

Neither educators nor noneducators want to hear or read a report that is filled with educational jargon. Over the years, education has developed numerous language "shortcuts"—words and phrases that most educators will recognize but that have no meaning for those outside the profession. Using educational jargon, even with other educators, runs the risk of not being fully understood. With the general public, educational jargon can prove disastrous, since the user seems to be talking snobbishly over the heads of his or her audience. Effective communicators speak directly, without lapsing into the "exclusive" language of their individual fields.

2. Learn to Be Yourself Before an Audience

Instead of attempting to create some largely imaginary public image, be yourself. Learn to relax before an audience. (Try taking three deep breaths before you get up to speak; it helps loosen that tight, anxious breathing and settle the butterflies in your stomach.) Smile. Don't be afraid to relate personal experiences and anecdotes when they coincide with the point of your report or speech. Sincerity and authenticity are endearing qualities that audiences will relate to and appreciate.

3. Learn to Key in on the Needs and Interests of Others

An important question for any speaker to ask is, What is it that my audience needs to hear? The flip side of the question is, What should I tell the audience? As a spokesperson, you speak for a group, not merely for yourself as an individual. What is the group communicating to the audience through you? How can that group need be structured to meet the needs and interests of the audience?

4. Learn to Limit the Scope of the Material Covered in Your Presentation

Limit the amount and intensity of information in both written and oral presentations. Don't try to inundate the reader/viewer. Where there is too much material to be covered comfortably, try structuring successive presentations or alternate speakers in order to create the variety needed to keep the audience actively interested. (In a written presentation, this variety is accomplished by dividing the material into chapters and subchapters, using visual devices such as dots and numbered lists—like this one—and incorporating diagrams and charts when appropriate.)

These four suggestions will ensure success if they are conscientiously and consistently applied to the task of fostering positive staff involvement in school management.

PLANNING FACTUAL PRESENTATIONS

The types of written presentations produced by school work groups vary considerably. They may be policy proposals, curriculum guides, teaching materials, or any number of other kinds of written product. Usually they do not follow the fairly standardized form of the business report.

On the other hand, experience has shown that regardless of the form of the product, it is likely that the producers—the staff group via its spokesperson—will be called upon to amplify the product. That is, the spokesperson will be asked to give some background about how the group gathered its information, what alternatives were considered by the group, and so on. This type of oral presentation may be given before other staff members (for instance, in a regular faculty meeting), before a curriculum committee at the district level, or before the board of education.

Since the report often is delivered before parents and the general public, including local news media representatives, it is especially important that the previous suggestions about being a successful spokesperson be followed. In addition to a speaker's background, adequate planning is essential to guaranteeing smooth, competent factual presentations of this nature.

Here are eight specific guidelines for planning factual presentations:

1. Material

Know what you want to say. Know your material well enough that you do not need to resort to notes except for certain key facts and statistics. Don't memorize a script, however. Reeling off a set piece looks amateurish, and it is impossible to maintain any continuity if you are interrupted.

2. Visual Aids

Don't be afraid to use good visual aids such as charts, diagrams, tables, and maps. Have them available, ordered, and ready-to-use without time lags that can turn into foot-shuffling agony for the audience. (More is discussed about choosing and using visual aids in the next section of this chapter.)

3. Speaker's Props

Make certain that everything you need for the presentation is *in place* and *working* before the time comes to make the presentation. Once you begin to speak to the audience, you don't want to find out that the microphone doesn't work or the projector bulb is burnt out. Make a checklist and use it well ahead of time.

4. Audience's Comfort

Either your own or someone else's previous experience with similar sorts of presentations should be able to guide you in selecting a suitable room in which to give the presentation. Avoid rooms that are too small and stuffy and, conversely, rooms that are cavernously large for a too-small audience. Check out the echo potential, too. Although often used for school presentations, gymnasiums are notorious for their echos, which can make the speaker inaudible or unintelligible. Try libraries, large classrooms, and off-school facilities as alternatives.

5. Dress

Look the part you plan to play. Every oral presentation is a bit like a stage play. Like it or not, part of how the audience responds to the speaker depends on the impression he or she creates visually. To create an image of competent authority, relatively conservative dress is the most acceptable form of attire for both men and women.

6. Voice

Sound like an authority. For both male and female speakers, the voice should be pitched a bit louder and a bit lower than normal. A high, breathy tone of voice conveys uncertainty and anxiety. For women in particular, a high-pitched, strident voice is unappealing and distracting to many listeners. Eleanor Roosevelt could get away with it; most people can't.

7. Carriage

Stand straight and keep your chin up. If a microphone is used, avoid catering to it. Have the microphones set so that you don't have to bend down to them in order to be heard. The correctly tuned and positioned microphone should be able to pick up your voice if you simply step up to the instrument and speak in a voice that is slightly louder than normal.

8. Discussion

Be prepared to answer questions. It is conventional at most presentations given by educators to open the forum up to audience questions at the conclusion of the formal presentation. Think ahead to possible questions, even to the extent of brainstorming them with the group and writing them down on paper. Then, be ready to answer the questions in an informed manner.

A good procedure during any question-and-answer period is to repeat the spectator's question. First, the repetition assures that you hear the question as the questioner intends it. Second, it allows the rest of the audience to hear the question clearly. (This is especially true in the case of large audiences where the speaker has a microphone but the questioner in the hall does not.)

By using the eight planning guidelines, the spokesperson who is charged with making a public or in-house presentation can be reasonably certain that the speaking responsibility will be successfully discharged. The speaker will enjoy a positive and confidence-building experience while, at the same time, the audience will be informed and will have opportunities to clarify anything that is in any way unclear.

CHOOSING AND USING VISUAL AIDS

Let's go back for a moment to the second guideline: using visual aids. Visuals can be a boon or a boondoggle, depending upon how they are chosen and used in the presentation.

Visuals most often used for educational presentations are slides, filmstrips, films, and overhead transparencies. They may be shown with the speaker narrating or, occasionally, with recorded narration. As anyone who has every used visual aids in any fashion knows, pitfalls abound.

Figure 6-2 shows some of the easiest pitfalls to avoid.

As can be seen from the items in Figure 6-2, most common visual-aid problems are preventable with a little foresight and common sense. An especially good idea is the speaker's trail run of the presentation. Like the actor's rehearsal, it helps smooth the presentation and avoid potentially disastrous pitfalls.

Using visual aids well also means choosing good visual aids to begin with. In Chapter Five, the section entitled "Illustrating Data Effectively" presented some suggestions for using bar graphs and pie charts. These and other types of illustrations can be effective for oral

Problem	*Prevention*
Dead projector bulb	Check bulb before the presentation. Have a spare bulb ready and know how to install it.
Screen image problems	Make a trial run before the presentation and modify plans accordingly.
Film/filmstrip threading difficulty	Set up the projector ahead of time with the film in place, so that it's just a matter of turning on the projector. Two films? Use two projectors and forget about threading and rewinding until after the presentation.
Misordered or shuffled slides/ transparencies	Again, a trial run helps. Place slides in containers, so that individual slides need not be touched again. Use transparency frames to keep flimsy transparencies from clinging and getting mixed up.
Room lighting problems	Know where the light switches are and have a colleague stand by, so that the speaker can stay with the projector.
Power problems	Fuses blow; know where the fuse box is and how to fix the situation. Check the power supply ahead of time to avoid overloading weak circuits.

FIGURE 6-2. Visual Aid Problems and Preventions

Problem	Prevention
Sight problems	Arrange room furniture to suit the presentation. Check on the condition of curtains and room-darkening shades.
Sound problems	Try out all sound equipment. Make certain that the sound level is appropriate. In an empty room, sound equipment may seem very loud but much of that sound is absorbed by an audience.
Safety problems	Be sure that exits are clear and marked. Loose power cords and speaker wires should be taped down, especially in walking areas.

FIGURE 6-2. (continued)

presentations as well as for written reports. The goals for these and all visual aids are worth restating here:

Clarity

Order

Interest

For visuals in the oral presentation setting, it is doubly important that the material be presented simply. Whether data are shown on transparencies or slides depends on the degree of sophistication of the visual-aid preparation. Slides are easier to store and more durable than transparencies; however, transparencies are easier and quicker to produce. For one-time presentations, the obvious choice is transparencies.

Overhead transparencies can be produced by several methods. The simplest is to draw directly onto the film with a grease pencil or transparency marker. More elaborate but also more professional-looking are transparencies that have been created by processing the film through a thermal copier. And there are newer copying machines on the market nowadays that will also create transparencies.

Because transparencies are used more than any other form of visual aid, the following guidelines may be useful:

- Select key words and fill in details through narration. (Put notes in the margin of the transparency frame to avoid having to juggle both the transparencies and separate presentation notes.)
- Make certain that all words are readable from the back of the room. Some authorities suggest using only six or seven words per line and about the same number of lines per transparency.
- Use a pointer placed on the stage of the projector, rather than turning your back and pointing to the screen image. The overhead projector is designed to allow the user to maintain better eye contact with the audience.
- Reveal points individually. Use a sheet of paper to cover items not being discussed at that moment. Turn the projector light off when changing transparencies. Eyes focus on light in a darkened room, so if the screen is lit it will get the attention, not the speaker. The speaker can and should control the focus of attention.

Many of the criteria above, reinforced by the characteristics of clarity, order, and interest, should be applied to the production and use of slides, films, and filmstrips.

PREPARING FOR "SPONTANEITY"

"Spontaneity" is a misnomer from an effective speaker's standpoint. Polished speakers are prepared for those moments when the presentation veers from the chosen path into the brambles of "off-the-cuff" questions and answers. They have thought ahead to possible questions and are prepared to answer them should they arise.

When the speaker senses that an audience is particularly interested in the proposed presentation, or when the presentation must cover a topic that is unusually broad and that can only be sketchily covered, it may be helpful to suspend the formal presentation and ask for audience questions from the start. Questions from the audience propel the presentation along lines of specific viewer interest. Audience participation is often heightened by this technique. Preplanning for the "spontaneity" on the speaker's part is the key to success in these instances.

THREE KEYS TO BEING AN EFFECTIVE SPOKESPERSON

Three vital keys to being an effective spokesperson are:

Preparation

An audience can tell when a speaker is unprepared, whether that unpreparedness comes in the form of a shaky oral delivery, poor visuals, or an inadequate room. Planning makes the difference between a mediocre and a superior presentation.

Presence

Top-notch speakers know what they're talking about. Their dress, bearing, and confidence contribute to the impression that they are experts in their chosen area. These speakers have high credibility in the eyes of the audience.

Personality

As important as presence, personality means that the speaker is authentic—a "real" person. He or she is capable of relating to an audience's interests and needs, and of giving his or her presentation a meaningful personal slant.

Remember these keys as the three P's: Preparation, Presence, and Personality. They add up to personal presentation skills that spell success.

Part Two

STAFF INVOLVEMENT: TRADITIONS AND INNOVATIONS

- Making Staff Meetings Meaningful
- How to Keep Your Advisory Boards On-Target and On-Task
- Quality Circles—Applying a New Form of Staff Involvement
- Developing Effective Staff Training Seminars
- Planning Workshops That Work
- Beyond Staff Involvement: Exploring the Concept of Shared Governance

Making Staff Meetings Meaningful

7

THE second half of *How to Build Staff Involvement in School Management* concentrates on specific staff-administration forms of interaction. Some of these are traditional, such as the staff meeting; others are more recent innovations in education, such as the quality circle (discussed in Chapter Nine).

The traditional staff meeting is an involvement forum with high potential. Successful staff or faculty meetings create understanding and awareness, and foster feelings of trust that can lead to increased staff productivity—e.g., volunteering for activity assignments, committee and task force work, and so on—and heightened morale.

However, the staff meeting also comes in for the lion's share of criticism. "Meetings are too long." "Too frequent." "Too short." "Dominated by the principal." "Dominated by vocal staff members." These wide-ranging criticisms point to one obvious conclusion: *There is no ideal staff meeting.*

Different staff personalities, leader styles, problems, objectives all require that the staff meeting form be flexible in order to meet the changing needs of both the staff and the administration.

This chapter will present ideas and techniques for keeping staff meetings flexible. While the context of most of the material focuses on building staffs (of all sizes and at all levels), it can also be generalized to include multibuilding staff meetings that might function under the direction of a "traveling" principal, or, more broadly, under the direction of the superintendent, the curriculum director, or other designated administrator.

ESTABLISHING A POSITIVE PATTERN

Staff involvement does not begin when the meeting begins. It starts much earlier. To establish a positive pattern of staff involvement, staff must be in on the planning operation.

As a starting point, find out when a staff meeting might be most conveniently held, and where. Time and place are often maintained as a matter of tradition long past the time when the original reasons for establishing this particular time or that specific place have been forgotten. Circumstances change. The first Tuesday of each month, say, may no longer be the convenient time it used to be, so why hold it sacred? The beginning of a new school year is a good time to query the staff about the best time and place for staff meetings.

Factors that may influence meeting times include extracurricular activities, bus schedules, seasonal events, part-time employment elsewhere, and personal commitments of staff members. These factors are especially true for meetings scheduled after the normal school workday, a traditional practice in many schools and, fortunately, now on the wane. Changing staff size and personal preferences may also motivate a desire to relocate the meeting place. With many schools declining in enrollment figures in recent years, shrinking staffs may want to move out of large cafeterias and libraries and into more intimate settings that allow for a cozier environment.

Whatever the desires of the staff regarding the time and place for staff meetings, those desires should be discovered and, as far as possible, followed. The scheduling and location of meetings is a matter of relatively small consequence, but one that can set a positive or negative tone for future staff-administration interaction.

Finding out how the staff feels about time and place is but the first step in a continuing process of discovering and meeting staff concerns and needs. The purpose of a staff meeting is to provide a forum for the discussion and resolution of problems and questions arising out of the business of education. Therefore, no topics are "off limits." Whatever is concerned with schooling—working conditions, student activities inside and outside the classroom, curricula, management planning, and so on—is fair game.

This is not to say that some topics might not be better handled in alternative forums. Contractual problems, for instance, have an established labor-management procedure in most cases. But no concern, either staff- or administration-generated, should be dismissed out of hand. Rather, pains should be taken at the staff meeting to redirect the problem to its more appropriate channel for resolution.

With this initial openness in mind, the survey technique suggested earlier might be adopted as a means of discovering topics for inclusion in future staff meetings. Figure 7-1 shows a typical, open-ended questionnaire that can be used to gain staff input into the staff meeting planning process.

STAFF MEETING TOPICS

Please answer the following questions and return this sheet to the office by 4:00 P.M. Friday, October 9.

What topics should be discussed at the *next* staff meeting?

What topics should be considered at staff meetings sometime in the future? When?

Should any previous topics be re-opened for discussion? Which?

Other comments?

FIGURE 7-1

Given anonymity, the pencil-and-paper survey can also serve as a barometer of school climate. This secondary function may be especially useful in larger schools, where the administrator is often somewhat removed from the day-to-day staff problems that are dealt with through assistant principals, counselors, and other support personnel. Likewise, such a survey can periodically put a superintendent in better touch with staff feelings throughout the district, regardless of the district's size. In fact, for the sake of good internal relations, a superintendent might be well advised to initiate some type of staff input survey as a regular means of tapping in on both teacher and administrator concerns throughout the school district.

Returning to the planning of the building staff meeting, it might be advantageous for large staffs to divide into groups for the planning process. Individual departments or groups of departments might meet informally to discuss potential items to be included in the meeting. This can be done in a brainstorming fashion or as shown by the survey suggested in Figure 7-1.

Potential discussion items should be transmitted in writing to the staff meeting coordinator. This person will be responsible for drawing up and publishing in advance of the meeting an agenda of topics to be considered. Figure 7-2 illustrates an appropriately detailed agenda.

ROOSEVELT XXXXXXXXXX SCHOOL
STAFF MEETING AGENDA

Meeting: Wednesday, January 12, 19____
        2:00 P.M.   **1**
        Room 202

  I. Review of December 15 minutes.   **2**

  II. Announcements
      A. PTSO Winter Carnival
         Mrs. Sprang
      B. Writing Assessment Results **3**
         Miss Bonner
      C. Other

  III. Reports
      A. Report Card Review Committee
         Mr. Johnson
      B. Vandalism Policy Task Force **4**
         Mrs. Evans

  IV. Old Business
      A. Summer School Course Offerings **5**

  V. New Business
      A. Monitoring Students During Fire Drills
      B. Do We Need a Second Reading Specialist? **6**
      C. Planning for Uniform Curriculum Guides
      D. Other

Attachment: Superintendent's Curriculum Directive

FIGURE 7-2

Note: If the building administrator is not the coordinator of the staff meeting—a possibility that is discussed in the next section of this chapter—then an effort must be made to include administrator input in the planning also. Similarly, student concerns, often generated out of the student council or some other representative group, should be considered in building the staff meeting agenda.

Figure 7-2 is number keyed as follows:

1. *Time and Place.* Since this staff meeting is scheduled for Wednesday the 12th, the agenda should be in the hands of the staff no later than Monday the 10th—preferably earlier, say, the previous Wednesday.

2. *Minutes of the previous meeting.* Minutes should have been printed and distributed to the staff already. Sometimes, minutes of one meeting are distributed with the agenda for the next. This is a mistake, since the events at the earlier meeting may influence the formation on the next meeting's agenda. Thus, it is a better strategy to distribute minutes as soon after the reported meeting as possible.

3. *Announcements.* Usually, announcements should be limited to items that cannot be easily transmitted through a daily bulletin or a printed message. These announcements may generate questions that can be answered immediately.

   It is handy to include an "Other" section that will allow for announcements to be given from the floor. These will be items of interest to the staff that have arisen too late to be included in the printed agenda.

4. *Reports.* This section is for the presentation of information coming out of committees and task forces. Similar to the announcements, though more extensive in character, these items are not open to discussion. Questions of a clarifying nature are appropriate.

   Both the announcements and the reports contain a listing that identifies the speaker. This identification serves as a helpful reminder to the speaker, the meeting leader, the staff audience, and the keeper of the minutes; it should be included regularly.

5. *Old Business.* Items of discussion held over from earlier meetings are included in this section. Perhaps a need for clarifying information suggested that the topic be retained "on the table" for a later meeting; or, perhaps the allotted time for the

earlier meeting expired before discussion of the item could be completed. There are a number of reasons for carrying over the discussion from one meeting to the next; however, it should be noted that the number of held-over items is—or, at least, should be—limited to one or two.

6. *New Business.* New business items are generated from staff surveys and discussions that have taken place to prepare the agenda. Concern about student behavior during fire drills has obviously inspired the first item. The second item is stated as a question with the idea that teachers can review in their own minds how they feel about the possibility of a second reading specialist.

Item C has apparently been created by a recent directive from the superintendent. Notice that a copy of the directive has been included so that the staff is fully informed.

Again, as for announcements, an "Other" section has been included to provide an immediate forum for urgent business that has come up between the time the agenda was produced and the actual meeting.

Establishing a positive pattern for staff meetings begins with making certain that the content of the agenda is generated out of the concerns of those who will be involved in the meeting and/or its outcomes. Staff input assures that staff members *can* play an active role in the meeting.

Further, by structuring the meeting as shown, items of business are taken up in a businesslike fashion. The order of business proceeds in a step-by-step manner that establishes a good working pattern, but the agenda also provides flexibility in that it allows for the introduction of unannounced items in those sections labeled "Other."

THREE USEFUL SCHEMES OF ORGANIZATION

Although the agenda, whether structured or adapted, sets the pattern for the staff meeting, there still remains to be decided *who* will carry out the pattern. In this sense, the organization of the staff meeting centers on the meeting leader, who directs the collection of staff, student, and administrator input, establishes or directs the making of the meeting agenda, and conducts the meeting itself. Consequently, this set of activities is the staff meeting *organization*, beyond the actual arrangement of the meeting itself (by means of the agenda).

This leadership role may be filled in three ways: (1) by an administrator—e.g., superintendent, principal, vice principal, etc.; (2) by a staff member; or (3) by a rotating roster of individuals.

Let's consider each of these three possibilities:

Administrative Leadership

Traditionally, staff meetings are conducted by an administrator, usually the school principal. This individual, either personally or through delegation, gathers staff input, sets the agenda, and conducts the meeting. If this person does his or her job conscientiously, the staff meeting will probably be successful. On the other hand, principal-directed staff meetings are sometimes seen as *principal-centered*. During periods of staff unrest (caused by personal animosities, unusual student problems, labor negotiations difficulties, staff cutbacks, or other exigencies), the administrator-directed staff meeting may be ineffectual. Some administrators may feel these are times when a firmer hand should be applied in the management of the school; however, just the opposite is usually more effective in restoring staff morale. The principal who relinquishes his or her traditional role as conductor of staff meetings is more likely to be seen as fair-minded and concerned than weak and vacillating, provided that he or she becomes an *active participant* in the meeting.

Staff Leadership

Asking a staff member to conduct the meeting is being done more often nowadays. The staff member may hold a particular leadership role, such as a department head, or may be designated especially to coordinate and conduct the staff meeting. Choosing an informal staff leader for this role can be an astute decision.

Often the staff member chosen is the head of a steering committee composed of staff and administrators for the purpose of considering school problems and developing agenda items for the larger staff meeting. This is particularly true in large schools, but it is often the case in smaller schools as well. The steering committee screens complaints, clarifies issues, and, in some cases, resolves problems before they are brought before the faculty forum in a full staff meeting.

It is only natural in cases where a steering committee exists that the committee's leader should also assume a leadership role in the staff meeting.

Effective staff leadership in this context depends on administrative support. It is important for this support to be both active and visible. For example, the principal cannot simply turn over the staff meeting to the steering committee head or some other staff member and then walk away. When this happens, failure of the staff meeting as a viable forum is virtually guaranteed, since the administrator is seen as "washing his hands of faculty problems." Consequently, the staff cannot expect that the administration will be sympathetic with or sensitive to their concerns. Hence, an almost unbridgeable gulf is created between staff and administration that will take considerable internal public relations to resolve to everyone's eventual benefit.

To avoid this potential problem, the principal or some other administrator must take an active—not dominant—part in the staff meeting. By assuming this secondary role, the administrator can still exert a degree of informal influence, as should be expected from the school leader, while at the same time demonstrating a desire to be constructively involved in positive interaction with the staff.

Shared Leadership

Rotating the role of staff meeting leader among two or more individuals can be a suitable compromise position between the two leadership modes outlined earlier. For instance, alternating the leadership role between the principal and the steering committee head is one possibility.

Rotating leadership demands more coordination, both among the various leaders and among the meeting planners. To provide for some feeling of security on the part of the staff, a certain degree of continuity should be maintained from meeting to meeting. Reasonable expectations of meeting parameters should be considered as constants. At the same time, different leaders should be able to bring their individual styles to the meeting.

In addition to sharing the burden of conducting staff meetings, the rotating leadership role allows for greater participation—directly in the leadership function—and encourages greater participation from other staff who react differently to the various leaders.

It is possible, too, to use the rotating idea in the other leadership modes. A principal and assistant principal may trade off. Similarly, the staff members of the steering committee may share the leadership function. Regardless of the configuration utilized, it is important to reiterate the need for continuity.

GUARANTEEING CONTINUITY

1. Develop a Schedule of Meeting Times and Places

If possible, this schedule should reflect a year's meetings and should be distributed well in advance of the first meeting. The time and place information should be generated from staff and administrator input. There's nothing wrong with changing from meeting to meeting, so long as the schedule reflects these changes.

Make sure that each person who is expected to attend the meetings has a schedule, and also post a schedule in the school office and/or the teacher workroom.

2. Develop a Standard Meeting Format or Agenda Form

Part of continuity is knowing what to expect from one meeting to the next. As illustrated in Figure 7-2, there should be provisions for follow-up from previous meetings—through minutes and reports—as well as advance notice of upcoming topics. The advance notice is accomplished by distribution of the agenda at least two days to a week prior to the staff meeting.

3. Develop Standard Meeting Procedures

Rules of action aid the flow of any meeting, regardless of the number of persons participating. A modified Robert's Rules format is desirable (see Appendix). In particular, the meeting procedure should distinguish between those items that are open to discussion and those that are presented for information only. For the most part, this distinction is accomplished by the position of the item on the agenda. The staff should also understand how staff meeting decisions will be treated—that is, what will be the level of authority? (Refer to "Orienting the Committee Compass" in Chapter One for a discussion of levels of authority.)

4. Develop a Record of the Meeting Through Clear Minutes

Minutes serve to report to the staff those actions of a substantive nature that were taken at the meeting and as an aid to planning future meetings. As a general rule, announcements and reports should be summarized briefly and the *action* taken on business items should be reported. It is unnecessary to report extensively on the discussion itself concerning old and new business, but rather to summarize clearly what was *done* with the item. Figure 7-3 illustrates sample minutes based on the meeting whose agenda is shown in Figure 7-2.

MINUTES

Staff Meeting of January 12, 19__

The meeting convened at 2:00 P.M. in Room 202. Principal Jane Sprang, presiding.

1. Minutes of the December 15 staff meeting were approved as printed.

2. Announcements

   2a. Mrs. Sprang announced that the PTSO Winter Carnival would be held in the gymnasium on Saturday, January 22. PTSO President John Warner will be coordinating the activity and a bulletin will be issued to the staff by Friday with details.

   2b. Responding to staff questions, Miss Bonner announced that the results of the recent student writing assessment were still being processed in the central office and would be available in three weeks, at which time she will ask for a special staff meeting.

   2c. There were no announcements from the floor.

3. Reports

   3a. Mr. Johnson reported that the Report Card Review Committee has begun gathering sample grade-reporting procedures from other schools and will be studying recent education journal articles as part of its review of the school's report card system. The committee's next meeting is scheduled for Monday, January 17, at 3:30 P.M. in Mr. Johnson's room (225). Non-committee members are invited to attend and provide input.

   3b. Mrs. Evans reported that the Vandalism Policy Task Force has completed its work and a written report will be distributed to the staff next week, along with a feedback questionnaire. The results of the questionnaire will be used to refine the final policy prior to presentation of the task force's report to the Board of Education next month.

FIGURE 7-3. Staff Meeting Minutes

4. Old Business

    4a. A printed listing of the course offerings for this year's summer school was distributed. The addition of Typing for Beginners was moved and carried. The entire list was then adopted and recommended for action by the administration.

5. New Business

    5a. It was moved and carried that during fire drills, those staff having planning period at that time should station themselves near the various exit doors to moniter student behavior during evacuation and re-entry of the building.

    5b. It was moved and carried to recommend to the administration that a half-time reading specialist be hired for next year to augment the work being done by Mrs. Robinson, the full-time reading specialist.

    5c. It was moved and carried that an interdepartmental task force be established to carry out the superintendent's directive regarding a uniform contents format for all subject area curriculum guides. It was further moved and carried that all department heads serve as the core of the task force with membership open to other concerned staff as well.

    5d. A motion from the floor to restrict student use of the athletic field during lunch periods was defeated.

Respectfully submitted,

Margaret Randall
Secretary to the Principal

FIGURE 7-3. (continued)

The format followed in Figure 7-3 presents the substance of the staff meeting in a clean, condensed form. The actions taken are clear and phrases such as "moved and carried to recommend" indicate the level of authority of the group decision. As was suggested, the announcements and reports are very briefly summarized, while the discussion of business items is completely omitted in favor of including only what was actually done. In item 5d, a failed motion is included. Some minutes report only successful motions, leaving out any mention of motions that are not carried.

The keeper of the minutes in this example is the principal's secretary. This person is an appropriate choice because of the secretarial skills involved, but another administrator or staff member might serve equally well. However, the individual who presides over the meeting should not have to take the minutes also.

ENCOURAGING ACTIVE PARTICIPATION

In addition to providing a suitable meeting structure carried out with competent leadership, here are some other suggestions for promoting active staff involvement:

- Focus on problems rather than on personalities. Keep the staff meeting looking for solutions, not scapegoats.
- Provide leadership in listening to all viewpoints, allowing sufficient time for staff members to think and formulate contributions to the discussion.
- Distribute reporting responsibilities widely, rather than to a select number of individuals; draw in newcomers and old-timers alike.
- Distribute background data ahead of time (with the agenda) so that staff members can be prepared for discussion topics.
- Encourage the sharing of expertise; bring and welcome outside resource people.
- Subgroup when appropriate to optimize opportunities for exchange of ideas.
- Provide times for summarizing and clarifying to keep discussion on target.
- For administrators specifically: Don't always have The Answer. Instead, interpret, mediate, comment, coordinate, and commend.
- Use verbal and nonverbal feedback that communicates acceptance and appreciation for contributions to the staff meeting.

GENERAL MEETINGS VERSUS SPECIALIZED MEETINGS

Most staff meetings tend to be general meetings. They cover a variety of topics based on current staff needs, follow up on previous concerns, or look ahead to future situations. The agenda and minutes (Figures 7-2 and 7-3) are for this type of staff meeting.

The general staff meeting is valuable for the very reason that it is general. It is designed to offer immediacy in dealing with current problems. Sometimes, however, there are specific topics to which an entire staff meeting should be devoted. Serious problems—a sudden rash of vandalism or a massive budget cut, for example—may give rise to a special meeting. Many of these problems are in the nature of an emergency and cannot be planned very far in advance. At the same time, there are special meetings that can be planned ahead of time so that certain topics can be treated more exhaustively.

Figure 7-4 lists some of the potential special meeting topics encountered in a typical school.

Topic	*Suggested Meeting Time*
Opening of School Review	Mid-September
Open House	September–October
Early Graduation	November–December
Graduation	April–May
Other special events (e.g., Homecoming, basketball season, academic awards night, etc.)	Two weeks–two months prior to the special event

FIGURE 7-4. Special Meeting Topics

Special meetings do not need to be long. In some cases, the meeting simply serves as a means of "touching base" with the staff, as in the case of the meeting to review the opening of school. It provides an opportunity to assess how the first few days have gone and to look for ways to make the opening week or two more successful in the future. Such a meeting might take only ten or fifteen minutes. However, other topics, such as graduation or awards night, may call for longer meetings.

By thinking ahead to the number and kinds of special meetings that will be needed, they can be included on the year-long schedule with the regular weekly or monthly general staff meetings.

ALTERNATIVES TO TRADITIONAL TIMES AND PLACES

We have all known schools that held staff meetings every week and others where once a year or once a semester was more the rule. How many staff meetings are needed or accepted depends on a number of factors. Here are three valuable questions to consider in determining the frequency of staff meetings:

1. What amount of time are staff members willing/able to commit to staff meetings?
2. How much can be accomplished at each meeting? How much needs to be accomplished?
3. Can some needs be met in other ways—i.e., through departmental or specialized meetings?

In answering these questions, it will help to view staff meetings less traditionally than perhaps they have been seen. The after-school staff meeting remains an absolute in many schools; however, if we are to increase the effectiveness of staff meetings, it will be essential to get rid of this pervasive stereotype. Asking staff to engage in a productive meeting after a tiring day of teaching sets the foundation for failure. Further, asking staff to remain past their normal leaving time markedly increases the likelihood that little or nothing of positive consequence will be accomplished at the meeting. It is hardly any wonder that many administrators complain that their after-school staff meetings are lackluster affairs that more often than not degenerate into bickering and complaining sessions. Staff meetings that fall into this pattern become morale-breakers rather than morale-builders.

What, then, are some alternatives?

First, consider the *time of day*. Before-school staff meetings are often an attractive option. They catch staff members while they are fresh—before the workday. And, since they fall between the teachers' starting time and that of the students, the duration of the meeting is automatically limited. This limitation is usually positive, since it increases the businesslike atmosphere and urges everyone to stay on-target in order to complete the agenda.

Another option is to schedule the staff meeting for some portion of the school day—usually for all or part of the afternoon—and to dismiss students accordingly. Numerous schools have this type of schedule already, so staff meetings can be held without the possibility of jeopardizing the mandatory number of teaching days required by local or state authorities. In this context, staff meetings take on an added dimension of importance. Often, staff meetings are viewed negatively from the teacher viewpoint as an add-on—something of marginal value that the administration requires. Placing staff meetings on the school calendar is often seen by staff as a sort of "putting your money where your mouth is" action on the part of the administration. There is something to be said for the attitude that if staff meetings really are important, they ought to be provided for within the school workday. During times of low morale among staff members, a change to this form of staff meeting can be most rewarding.

Second, consider the *place.* Is it essential to meet in the same room every time? Must staff meetings be held in the school at all? Large faculties are more limited in this respect than smaller staffs, because often there is only one suitable facility within the school for the large staff. Small staffs, on the other hand, can get away from the cafeteria or library setting and simply meet in a classroom. And, they can move around the school, using a variety of classrooms over the course of the school year. Elementary schools are ideal in this respect, and the "tour" allows teachers to see how others arrange their rooms and so on.

Moving off the school premises is another way of introducing variety to the staff meetings and giving staff a chance simply to get out of the school setting and into a more relaxed environment. Nearby facilities may include restaurant private rooms (often standing empty during most of the day) and hotel or motel meeting rooms. Often, these rooms can be used free of charge, because the management looks upon the school's use of the room as a public service gesture designed to promote goodwill. Usually civic buildings and banks also have meeting rooms that can be scheduled at little or no cost. For very small staffs, the home of a teacher or administrator who lives in the school neighborhood may be a possible meeting site.

Yet another alternative to the traditional staff meeting is the ongoing staff meeting: a continuous, day-long meeting, where the staff participates during one of its planning periods. The meeting lasts all day; the participants change from period to period. Obviously, there are some limitations to this form of staff meeting. It is suited best to secondary schools or elementary schools where staff members have one or two free periods during the day. Also, since only part of the faculty is present at any one time, the meeting cannot cover any extensive agenda very effectively.

The ongoing meeting, however, is well-suited to a single-issue agenda. It provides an opportunity to discuss an issue in depth in a small group setting and, at the same time, allows input from the whole staff by the close of the day. Ideas, conclusions, and recommendations of each group can be passed along to the next by the meeting coordinator, usually a principal, assistant principal, or counselor whose time schedule is flexible. (Indeed, here is an excellent opportunity for shared leadership among the administrative, support, and teaching staffs.)

A final alternative is the voluntary staff meeting. Most staff meetings are required or quasi-required. One way to find out how valuable staff meetings are considered by the staff is to make attendance strictly voluntary. The results can be interesting.

PREPLANNING AND POSTPLANNING

Staff meetings are a bit like the familiar potato chip advertisement: You can't stop at just one! So, it is best to think of staff meetings as an ongoing commitment that requires a preplanning stage (i.e., gathering information on which to base or plan the agenda) and a postplanning stage (wherein the planner asks, "Have I done everything that is necessary to make the staff meeting successful?").

The successful staff meeting planner/presenter should ask him- or herself:

1. Have I included in the agenda all that needs to be reported to or discussed by the staff?
2. Does the agenda include follow-up items from previous staff meetings?
3. Do I understand the impact and level of authority connected with each item?
4. Am I familiar with the proper procedures for conducting the meeting?
5. Is the amount of material appropriate to the time allotted?
6. Do I understand which items can be carried over if necessary and which items must be dealt with immediately?
7. Am I prepared to be assertive in keeping the discussion on-task?
8. Are physical arrangements (room, heat, light, seating, audio-visual equipment) taken care of?

9. Is there a back-up plan in the event that the meeting cannot proceed according to plan?

10. Have I asked myself: "What else?"

By working conscientiously, the school leader can develop appropriate strategies that will ensure meaningful staff meetings.

How to Keep
Your Advisory Boards
On-Target and On-Task

8

THE advisory board composed of staff members is an involvement forum of long standing in education, although it may have a variety of names. Some schools use the term *steering committee*, while others may use the title *principal's cabinet.* Essentially, advisory boards are committees rather than task forces, because they exist mainly to *review* policies, problems, and situations, and to *recommend* appropriate action to the administration.

The functions *review* and *recommend* will be focused upon in this chapter.

DEFINING ADVISORY BOARD PURPOSES

In most cases, advisory boards are established to serve as faculty sounding boards. The principal brings to the group any number of matters for consideration, ranging from building security to curriculum and instruction. Subject matter limits are fairly broad and any constraints that do exist stem primarily from contractual agreements and higher-level policy (i.e., rules and regulations promulgated by the board of education).

The purpose of an advisory board is to review school matters and to recommend appropriate action to the board's supervisor.

Figure 8-1 lists some of the kinds of school matters that may come to the attention of a staff advisory board.

Staff Matters
Placement and transfer, except as delineated in labor agreements
Room and teaching assignments
Supervision and evaluation
Inservice training

Curricular Matters
Curriculum planning
Instructional techniques and technologies
Text adoption, equipment purchase and use

Management and Facility Matters
Building maintenance and renovation
Transportation
Communications (e.g., intercom use, bulletins, school mail system)
Scheduling
Attendance and other recordkeeping

Student Matters
Credit requirements, except as limited by district policy
Activities, both in school and extracurricular
Groups and projects (e.g., clubs, student council)
Special problems, discipline, vandalism, etc.
Support services (e.g., counseling, testing, special education)

External Matters
Public relations
District budget, program funding, etc.
Parent and other community groups (e.g., PTA, "booster" clubs)

FIGURE 8-1. Advisory Board Subjects

Although the framework of this chapter (and reflected in **Figure 8-1**) is concerned mainly with advisory boards that function in individual schools, the broader worth of such groups should also be recognized. Other staff involvement opportunities that use the advisory board concept are:

1. A *superintendent's cabinet.* Composed of staff members from throughout the district, this group will aid in keeping the superintendent and other "central office" administrators in touch with staff concerns and viewpoints.

2. A *curriculum and instruction advisory committee.* Supervised perhaps by the district's curriculum director, this committee can be useful in developing a coordinated curriculum planning program. Likewise, in larger school districts utilizing subject-matter-specific administrators—e.g., Language Arts Supervisor, Art Supervisor, Music Supervisor—separate subject area committees will be helpful.

3. A *facilities review committee.* This committee can serve to put the building and grounds manager in touch with staff concerns and plans.

4. *Special project advisory boards.* This board serves to promote smoother dissemination of project materials and to aid in coordinating activities in individual buildings and/or subjects and grade levels.

All of these types of advisory boards can be structured similarly, each using the criteria for staff involvement that was discussed in Chapter One. Perhaps it will be valuable to repeat an element of that discussion here by reiterating the importance of these six questions:

- *What* is the job of the advisory board?
- *Who* can do that job best?
- *When* will the work take place?
- *Where* will the board meet?
- *Why* is the board's effort needed?
- *How* will the board's advice be used?

The school leader who answers these questions carefully at the outset is most likely to build an advisory committee that is capable and willing to stay on-target and on-task.

REVIEWING LEVELS OF AUTHORITY

An advisory board is intended to function at the middle level of authority, that of *recommendation*. Groups that function at the lower level, *information*, are not, strictly speaking, *advisory*, since such groups provide only information and not "advice." Groups that function at the highest level, *decision*, are not advisory in character either. These groups might be more appropriately called management teams —or management task forces—because they do more than merely advise; they act. That is, they *make* decisions as opposed to recommending decisions.

Staff members who participate in an advisory board need to understand the level of authority at which the board functions. Since an advisory board is essentially a committee structure, it is possible to proceed from some of the ideas presented in Chapter One; however, there are some important differences that must also be taken into account. These differences distinguish the committee which is formed for a single purpose (see Chapter One) and the committee—the advisory board—which must consider many issues on an ongoing basis. Seen in this light, the advisory board is a fairly classic example of the so-called "standing committee."

The long-term commitment of an advisory committee makes it necessary to formulate a set of rules, or bylaws. They act to set the parameters within which the advisory board must operate, to orient new board members—since, as with any long-term group, membership is likely to change over a period of time—and to ensure a degree of continuity.

Figure 8-2 is a sample set of rules governing an advisory board's work.

Let's examine the advisory board, as shown in Figure 8-2.

First, this is a small board of four members, an appropriate size for a school of ten to forty staff members. These board members are elected by their peers; however, in practice, it is possible that individual staff members may volunteer to stand for election. This is a customary procedure that preserves both the voluntary aspect of committee participation and the democratic opportunity to recognize peer talents. The leadership role is shared by each of the four board members on a rotating basis.

Second, the board may consider all issues that are germane to the school. These issues may be generated from within the school—i.e., by

---

ROOSEVELT XXXXXXXXXXX SCHOOL

Advisory Board

Meeting Times: Monthly, on the third Tuesday, 3:15 P.M.

Membership: Four staff members, each serving on a rotating basis as chairman of the group. Members to be elected annually at the opening of school by the staff at large.

Goal: To consider school issues brought to the board's attention by other staff members, administrators, students, parents, or other concerned citizens, and to advise the administration as to appropriate courses of action.

Functions:
1. To gather information about school-community concerns, both incidentally and deliberately.
2. To gather information of a collateral nature in order to assess such concerns accurately.
3. To report findings and recommendations (a) to the concerned parties and (b) to the administration for administrative action.
4. To conduct periodic staff meetings coordinated with the administration in order to create staff forums on specific concerns prior to recommending any particular action on those concerns.

Limitations:
1. The advisory board may not consider matters outside the scope of the school.
2. The advisory board may not consider matters which are not governed by the school.
3. The advisory board may gather information only for its own considerations.
4. The advisory board may not make policy or decisions but shall advise in their making.

FIGURE 8-2. Advisory Board Rules

staff, administrators, or students—or from external sources. However, these issues must not be governed by bodies outside the school. For example, the board may advise on scheduling student lunch periods but not on setting school lunch prices. Scheduling is a prerogative of the school, whereas lunch prices are normally established by the district (i.e., the board of education).

Third, the board has authority to, and in fact is limited to, gathering information for its consideration. In other words, the advisory board may not be used simply as a research group by the school administration, the staff union, or others. And, the advisory board may conduct staff meetings—either in place of or in addition to the regular staff meetings—for the purpose of considering certain issues in a staff forum. Finally, the board may advise, but it may not make decisions or policy.

In developing a well-functioning advisory board, members and prospective members must thoroughly understand the group's functions and limitations. To this end, it seems only reasonable to develop and publish some form of "rules" for all staff members. There are many variations of the suggestions given for rules in Figure 8-2, but any set of rules should include: meeting time and frequency (and place, if a regular meeting place is to be used), membership, goal(s), functions, and limitations.

DEVELOPING APPROPRIATE GROUP STRUCTURES

Because an advisory board is a form of committee, there is no reason that such a board cannot utilize the three committee structures suggested in Chapter One. Whereas most committees will form one type of organization to use throughout the life of the committee, the advisory board, acting in the manner of a *standing committee*, may have recourse to all three organizational structures, using each one as it deems appropriate for the specific task at hand.

For this reason, it is suggested that the advisory board adopt the *circular model* as its "core" organization. That is, the board in most instances will function as a total group, and action will center on group discussion of issues and group decisions about recommendations to be forwarded to the administration.

As the complexity of an issue may warrant it, a more complex organization should be adopted for a limited time, until that particular issue is dealt with. As illustrated in Chapter One, two more complex forms of committee organization are the *linear model* (Figure 1-4), in which the group works through a series of subgoals toward the main goal, and the *modular model* (Figure 1-5), in which the group breaks into smaller subgroups in order to work separately on individual subgoals. In the modular form of organization, a coordinator or coordinating group synthesizes the findings of the various subgroups and processes all the information for consideration by the total body.

Full use of the modular structure, however, may be limited by the number of advisory board members. In general, advisory boards tend to have fewer than ten members, which limits viable subgrouping. (Some "subgroups" are likely to consist of a single individual.) At the same time, viability of the subgrouping option must be weighed against the advantages inherent in small committees. Such committees, in the long run, tend to operate more efficiently than large committees. Where a standing committee is involved, this aspect of continuous efficiency may favor sacrificing the option of extended subgrouping. Of course, some subgrouping will still be possible even with a small advisory board. The four-member board suggested by the rules illustration (Figure 8-2) could still find appropriate opportunities to break some large issue into more workable bits by dividing into teams of two.

SUBGROUPING OPTIONS

How can the advisory board assure adequate representation of the total staff?

In small schools where staff members are likely to be familiar with each other's concerns and interests, it is appropriate to elect advisory board members at large—that is, representing the entire staff. But what about advisory boards in larger schools, some so large that some staff members rarely meet and scarcely know colleagues?

In larger schools, the answer is not merely to increase the size of the advisory board; rather, it is to subgroup for the purpose of electing advisory board members in the first place. In this way, some measure of total representation can be assured by providing that each elected member comes from a specific constituency.

Figures 8-3, 8-4, and 8-5 illustrate sample subgrouping options for (1) a large elementary school, (2) a middle or junior high school, and (3) a high school.

In Figure 8-3, the twenty-two staff members are divided into four subgroups, either by close grade level or, in D, as various specialists. The board is comprised of four members, one from each subgroup.

Note: This figure conforms to that of Figure 8-2, where the example could easily be "Roosevelt Elementary School."

Subgroup Description	Number of Staff	Number of Board Members
A. Grades K–2	6	1
B. Grades 3–4	5	1
C. Grades 5–6	6	1
D. Reading specialist, librarian, speech therapist, art specialist, music specialist	5	1
Total Advisory Board		4

FIGURE 8-3. Elementary School Advisory Board Constituencies

Subgroup Description	Number of Staff	Number of Board Members
A. Language arts, foreign languages	8	1
B. Social studies, reading	6	1
C. Mathematics, science	8	1
D. Music, art, home economics, industrial arts	9	1
E. Physical education, special education	9	1
F. Librarian, counselor, speech therapist, business and typing teachers, work-study director	6	1
Total Advisory Board		6

FIGURE 8-4. Middle or Junior High School
Advisory Board Constituencies

In Figure 8-4, the forty-six member staff is represented by six individuals on the advisory board. The constituencies are grouped by related subject areas wherever possible. (Group F is the exception, being a kind of catchall for staff not included in the other groups.) The size and configuration of this figure is typical of many junior high and middle schools. Although many middle schools are not strictly departmentalized, they may prefer to arrange their subgroups in this fashion. Or, they may prefer the elementary style arrangement shown in Figure 8-3. Yet another option for middle schools is to subgroup in the same manner that the school is subgrouped if, for instance, the staff is divided into "houses" or "schools-within-schools."

In any case, the subgroups should be related in a way close to the natural relationships of the staff, and they should be structured to contain approximately the same number of persons. As can be seen in Figure 8-4, each subgroup contains from six to nine members.

Subgroup Description	Number of Staff	Number of Board Members
A. English/language arts	8	1
B. ESL, foreign languages	6	1
C. Social studies	10	1
D. Mathematics	8	1
E. Science	8	1
F. Art, music, drama	7	1
G. Special education	8	1
H. Physical education	7	1
I. Vocational and business teachers, driver education	9	1
J. Home economics, industrial arts	10	1
K. Librarians, reading, speech, counselors	7	1
Total Advisory Board		11

FIGURE 8-5. High School Advisory Board Constituencies

In Figure 8-5, the staff of eighty-eight is represented by an eleven-member board. As with the middle and junior high school example, the subgroups have been formed by pooling staff members in related curricular areas. A smaller advisory board certainly could be achieved by making each subgroup larger, but eleven members is a reasonable size and need not be reduced at the risk of losing some of the representative capacity of the larger group.

These examples are based on actual school staff rosters and are fairly typical of a cross section of American public schools. Each school, however, can be expected to have its own grouping problems. Some may have larger vocational staffs, more extensive foreign-language programs, or a higher percentage of special education teachers. These individual characteristics will influence the content of the school's subgroups and, consequently, the make-up of the advisory board.

TAKING ADVANTAGE OF
SKILL-BUILDING OPPORTUNITIES

The advisory board provides opportunities for group skill-building, particularly in areas of teamwork and problem solving. Astute administrators will recognize the potential educational value for advisory board staff and will capitalize on that potential in the following ways:

1. By providing group leadership when appropriate;
2. By being candid about administrative concerns, constraints, and prerogatives; and
3. By appropriately recognizing advisory board recommendations and following board advice when appropriate.

The school administrator will be called upon to provide leadership, not only in structuring the advisory board—both in terms of membership and in setting parameters—but also in "getting the ball rolling" at the start of each school year. The administrator must actively initiate the board anew annually, since the board functions under the administrator's supervision. Therefore, the administrator gives leadership at the start in all cases. But more may be needed. Because members are elected to the advisory board, the board may desire to call upon the administrator to provide some sort of leadership training for members. In many instances, this call for assistance will not be overt, and the administrator will need to sense when to lend a hand. Likewise, the administrator needs to be sensitive to those times when the board needs to be left alone so as to avoid any taint of outside influence.

The value of advisory boards will also be enhanced if the administrator develops an atmosphere of trust by being candid about the concerns held by him- or herself and other administrators regarding certain issues; by letting the board know about any constraints the administration must work within; and by making clear what issues (or aspects of issues) are within his or her prerogatives to do something about. This openness with the board will strengthen communication and will help the board come to realistic decisions about on-target recommendations.

This ''cards on the table'' honesty also applies to treatment of the advisory board's recommendations. If the recommendation is of merit, it should be put into effect by the administrator. If it is not, the administrator should communicate to the board his or her reasons for not adopting the recommendation. And, regardless of whether or not the board's recommendation is utilized, it is important that the administrator recognize the thought and effort that went into each member's service on the board.

Whether recognition comes in the form of a certificate, a letter of appreciation, a faculty dinner honoring the board members, or in some other fashion, such acknowledgment of service demonstrates that the advisory board is a distinct and valuable body. It reinforces the notion that staff can be meaningfully involved in school management without *being* school management, which is an important distinction.

EXTENDING THE GROUP BEYOND THE SCHOOL

Throughout this book, the term *staff* has been used to mean a school's faculty and support personnel (e.g., librarians, counselors, various specialists), those who work with or directly for students. But there are also other school employees who may contribute to an advisory board. These include the custodial and maintenance personnel, cafeteria workers, bus drivers, and others who work closely with administrators and/or staff members. Many schools include representatives of this extended staff on their advisory boards, keeping in mind that such persons, in addition to working for the school, are often parents and community members who have a stake in the smooth operation of their educational institutions.

Likewise, many schools are opening advisory boards to the community, drawing in both parents and nonparents. This is particularly true in communities that still function with neighborhood schools, but it is being attempted in large cities as well in a move to counteract some of the disadvantages of busing and neighborhood fragmentation caused by so-called "magnet" schools. An example might be a fine arts school where students with special interests and aptitudes would be drawn from all city neighborhoods. In another part of town, an industrial trades school might similarly draw students from throughout the city to study auto mechanics, welding, or similar courses.

An all-too-common situation that works against the effectiveness of advisory boards, however, is the maintenance of separate staff and citizen boards. I would advocate the merging of these separate boards, even at the risk of forming a rather large body, in order to share the advisory function fully and to promote a truer meeting of school and community minds.

While separate staff and citizen advisory boards may mitigate some conflict and simplify some problems, they are more likely to create divisiveness. Pooling into one advisory board, although it may sharpen some issues, will more likely result in better understanding of the school's problems by the community and of the community's concerns by the staff. In this context a successful advisory board can be a strong public relations builder.

SIX STEPS TO A SUCCESSFUL ADVISORY BOARD

1. *Define the goals and purposes of the advisory board.* Make sure that board members know which topics come within the group's purview and which topics do not.

2. *Be certain the group understands that its level of authority is the recommendation level.* The advisory board role is to consider and advise, not merely to gather information on the one hand or to make decisions on the other.

3. *Develop a representative structure.* In larger schools designate staff subgroups so that board members have a constituency and all staff members are fairly represented.

4. *Help the advisory board build appropriate skills.* By providing good leadership, school administrators can help to devel-

op better group work and problem-solving skills that will enhance the board's functioning.

5. *Build trust by recognizing the board's value.* Use positive reinforcement by adopting board recommendations when appropriate and by commending board service.

6. *As the need arises, extend the board beyond the school staff.* As a means of involving the extended staff and providing a school–community interaction forum, the advisory board can be a positive morale-building and public relations vehicle in addition to providing for solid staff involvement in school management.

Following these six steps will ensure that the school administrator builds an advisory board that stays on-target and on-task.

Quality Circles— Applying a New Form of Staff Involvement

THE quality circle concept, which in recent years has become a hot item in business management, is now making some headway in school management. As a vehicle for building staff involvement, a quality circle offers yet another tool for the effective school leader.

This chapter capsulizes the quality circle concept and its history, and outlines how school leaders can make one or more quality circles part of their management profile.

CHARACTERISTICS OF A QUALITY CIRCLE

The quality circle concept originated in Japan during the 1960s as a means of involving workers in the upgrading of industrial products. Before World War II and immediately after, Japanese products were regarded as low-quality, cheap goods. In order to compete successfully in world markets, the Japanese industrialist was compelled to improve radically both the quality and international image of Japanese goods.

At the same time, another factor enters into the industrial picture: the Japanese company family. In Japan, unlike in the United States, workers are more likely to retire from the company in which they begin their careers. Companies in Japan have often been characterized as corporate families. This is not to say that in most cases these "families" have been run democratically; in fact, in many ways Japanese companies are more autocratic than those in the West. Nonetheless, Japanese industrial leaders recognized the importance of involving workers in the problem-solving/decision-making process in order to create the quality revolution that has, indeed, taken place over the past twenty years in Japanese manufacturing.

Based on the efforts of Japanese industry, the quality circle has recently been recognized as a viable staff involvement tool for school managers. The concept can be defined as follows:

A quality circle is a structured group approach to problem identification and solution.

Casting the quality circle in the context of staff involvement also means that it must be viewed in relation to the committee and the task force. It may be best to think of the quality circle as a sort of midpoint between these two traditional staff involvement structures. But, while the quality circle embodies aspects of both the committee and the task force, it is neither a built-up version of one nor a watered-down version of the other. The quality circle is a distinct staff involvement structure.

Here's how a quality circle may be characterized:

1. Structure and Membership

Ideally, a quality circle is a homogeneous group of five to fifteen individuals. With the exception of the circle leader, participation is voluntary. The group meets on a regular basis—often weekly or semi-weekly—and usually in a full-group setting. Most problem solving is conducted by the full group—i.e., using the circular model of organization (see Figure 9-1) rather than subgrouping.

2. Pre-/Post-Activities

Preliminary training is essential to the effective functioning of any quality circle. Typically, this training consists of thorough orientation to the quality circle concept, instruction in problem-solving techniques, and training in *affective* communication.

Following the activities of the circle, attention is given to follow-up on circle decisions and/or recommendations, evaluation of the problem-solving process, and reinforcement/reward. Satisfaction and a sense of accomplishment, often coupled with public recognition, are usually considered ample staff reward for active involvement in a quality circle. Monetary rewards are seldom given, although released

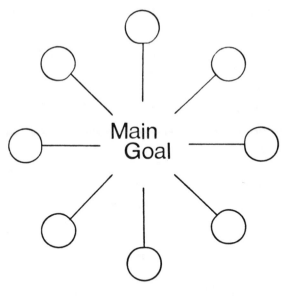

FIGURE 9-1

time from teaching or other duties may facilitate circle meetings during school hours.

3. Scope and Authority

In most instances, circles select their own problems. They are not expected to take on all problems and will recognize when certain problems should be dealt with administratively through the teacher union, a special committee, or a task force. Part of the pre-activity training for quality circles will be focused on developing selection criteria for choosing which problems are within the scope of the circle.

Quality circles may function at any of the three levels of authority that have been previously identified. However, circles that function at the highest level, that of *decision*, will have the most effectiveness. (*Note:* "Effectiveness" means the staff will be involved to the greatest degree and communication will increase, not necessarily that the "best" decisions will be generated. Good decisions are more likely to be the result of understanding and thorough training rather than the product of any particular level of authority.)

HOW CIRCLES IMPROVE COMMUNICATION

A prime benefit of the quality circle is its service as a vehicle for improved intraschool communication. In establishing a quality circle, the school leader (typically the building principal) accomplishes the following:

1. *Builds trust.* Staff are willing to work toward educational goals when they are given the chance to do so.

2. *Recognizes staff knowledge and experience.* This recognition strengthens educational professionalism.

3. *Decentralizes the decision-making process.* By allowing and encouraging staff to make decisions in specific areas, administrators activate staff competencies and, at the same time, free themselves for other chores.

4. *Builds unity and strengthens morale.* Staff and administration adopt the viewpoint that the school is a cooperative venture in an era too often characterized by the competitive nature of labor-management relations.

SOME OTHER BENEFITS

In addition to improving staff–administration communications, the quality circle has many other benefits, not the least of which is the circle's stated goal: to identify and solve problems.

Because the circle focuses on problems "close to home"—that is, within the expertise of the group—it has the advantage of intimate knowledge that can lead to earlier, more equitable solutions. Quality circle participants, trained in problem-solving strategies, are able to use this knowledge by channeling it through the open communication system of the circle and to develop innovative approaches to potential solutions.

James S. Bonner, who introduced the quality circle concept to the Muskegon, Michigan, public schools, says that the key to effective innovation or change is a willingness on the part of staff and administration to see their own strengths and weaknesses, and then to change for the better. Bonner has explored the quality circle concept for educators in several articles.[1] His work in training, reading, and consulting has led to the conclusion that successful change is the product of successful human interaction.

Thus, it is fair to list the quality circle's main objective of problem solving as a benefit of the circle and not simply as its aim.

---

[1] James S. Bonner, "Applying Japanese Management Strategies to Educational Management," *Michigan School Board Journal*, December 1981, and "Japanese Quality Circles: Can They Work in Education?" *Phi Delta Kappan*, June 1982.

Some other benefits of quality circles are reported as follows:

- Increased understanding by staff of management problems and constraints.
- Increased understanding of staff concerns by management.
- Increased mutual respect between staff and administration.
- Reduced conflict between staff members and between staff and administration.
- Eliminated some negative attitudes held by staff members.
- Increased feelings of accomplishment.

TAPPING STAFF KNOWLEDGE

The key to success with a quality circle begins with recognizing strengths and weaknesses. Discovering and understanding limitations will assure that groups are formed which can successfully accomplish their designated tasks.

This process of targeting can be aided by having the staff answer these questions:

1. What will the quality circle do?
2. Who will decide which problems can be tackled by the circle and which are better referred elsewhere?
3. Is the building administrator supportive of trying the quality circle concept?
4. Are others interested and supportive: the superintendent? the curriculum director? the teacher union?
5. Are staff members open to try the circle concept?
6. Can volunteers be found to participate in the circle?
7. Is there someone who can provide leadership in establishing a quality circle? In providing in-service training?
8. Will this same person or someone else serve as circle facilitator?
9. What kinds of competencies are needed by the circle? Who can provide them?
10. When and where and how often will the circle meet?
11. Is released-time support available for teaching staff, or must circle meetings be conducted outside school hours?

12. How will circle participants know at which level of authority they will operate?
13. How will circle plans/solutions be implemented?
14. Who will judge the effectiveness of the circle?
15. What will be the evaluative criteria? Who establishes the criteria?

By answering these and related questions early in the formation of a quality circle, it will be possible to approach the project with open eyes.

FORMING THE CIRCLE

Figure 9-2 provides a step-by-step process for initiating a quality circle.

STEP ONE—Awareness

The impetus for a quality circle should come from the staff. However, in order for the staff to desire to form a quality circle, individuals must be aware that quality circles are an option. Therefore, it is essential that some time be given to developing an awareness of the quality circle concept.

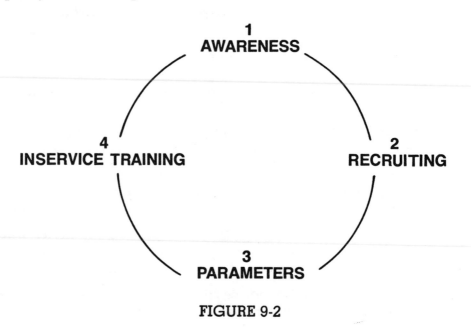

FIGURE 9-2

Awareness can be created in several ways:

1. *Through brochures and hand-outs.* School leaders can utilize established publications or create their own informational materials to introduce the circle concept to staff. Posters in the faculty lounge and coordinated information releases with the teacher union can also help to get the word out about quality circles.

2. *Through structured in-service training.* Making quality circles a topic of in-service education can spur staff members to implement circles in their own areas.

3. *Through personal examples.* Persons already involved in quality circles may be invited to a faculty meeting to discuss their experiences. These people may be from within the same school or district, or from neighboring districts. If a principals' circle has been formed as a management team device, then principals themselves can cite personal experience in talking to their own staffs. This is likely to be the case in larger districts where the quality circle is being tried as a "middle management" problem-solving tool before being introduced to other employee levels.

4. *Through business examples.* Community business people can also be used as resources. Even though quality circles in the business sector differ from educational quality circles, the common points are such that using business examples is extremely viable. In addition, involving business people will help to enhance school–community relations, particularly as business begins to see that education faces many of the same sorts of problem-solving and communication dilemmas.

Utilizing staff involvement to create an awareness of the quality circle's potential as a problem-solving tool will encourage staff members to investigate the possibility of starting quality circles in their own areas.

STEP TWO—Recruiting

When staff members take full initiative, little actual recruiting may be necessary. In many cases, however, one or two staff members may broach the subject of a quality circle to the administrator. In this instance, once the go-ahead to form the circle is given, it will be necessary to recruit members for the circle.

Recruiting is best accomplished through personal contact. The administrator in charge may initiate such contact with other staff members, or, sometimes more effective, those staff members already interested in circle formation may contact their peers.

Effective recruiting combines several characteristics:

- Illustrating potential for change and betterment. The question to be answered is, "What will a quality circle do for me, my department, my school, etc.?"
- Demonstrating the acceptability of this mode of problem solving. "Will the administration, union, department, etc., agree to the use of a quality circle?"
- Reinforcing the need for participation. "Why is my input sought? Why am I important to the process?"

In most cases, when these questions are answered to individual staff members' satisfaction, the recruiting effort will readily bear fruit and volunteers will be plentiful. Staff commitment arises from a professional awareness that problems exist to which solutions can be found. If the staff are allowed and encouraged to find those solutions, they will gladly volunteer to try the quality circle approach.

STEP THREE—Parameters

As discussed earlier, the bounds of a quality circle must be established at the very beginning, so that staff members know what they may and may not do. These parameters can best be described in terms of *scope* and *authority*. Circle participants must know the scope of their involvement—that is, which topics come within the specified goal(s) of the circle—and the level of authority at which the group operates. The most effective circles operate at the *decision* level within closely prescribed limitations.

Figure 9-3 gives a capsule description of an English Department quality circle operating at the high school level.

Notice in the example in Figure 9-3 that the group has the authority to make decisions, but only in the areas where circle members are directly affected. In other situations, where the circle decision overlaps into another field (for example, a scheduling decision that also affects the Social Studies Department), the circle decision is taken to be a recommendation only.

Also notice that the circle is specifically prohibited from discussing topics that would normally fall either into the realm of manage-

I. **Goals**
   A. To allow staff members to develop solutions to intradepartmental problems, including scheduling, text selection, curriculum development, and other problems.
   B. To improve communication among English Department members.

II. **Membership**
   A. Circle membership is open to all staff in the English Department, both professional and paraprofessional.
   B. Participation is voluntary.

III. **Leadership**
   A. Circle leaders are chosen by the group.
   B. The circle leader may be a professional or paraprofessional working in the English Department.

IV. **Meetings**
   A. The circle will meet semi-weekly for one hour.
   B. A schedule of meetings will be established by the group for planning purposes.

V. **Authority**
   A. Circle decisions may affect only circle members or have the consent of others affected.
   B. Decisions will be recognized by the administration and implemented accordingly.

VI. **Limitations**
   A. Circle decisions are limited to subjects affecting only members of the English Department.
   B. Decisions which overlap into other departments shall be considered as recommendations only.
   C. The circle will not discuss topics involving:
      1. Salaries and benefits
      2. Hiring, probation, and dismissal policies
      3. Personalities

FIGURE 9-3. English Department Quality Circle

ment prerogative or into the arena of labor–management negotiations. Likewise, the often negative area of personalities is avoided by this prohibition.

By establishing the "do's and don't's" of the quality circle, it will be possible to initiate an effective, on-target working group.

STEP FOUR—In-service Training

Before getting into the "real work" of the circle, a period of in-service training should be pursued along two lines: communication and problem solving.

Training in communication should center on group dynamics and interaction, affective communication (feelings and body language as well as words), and modeling behaviors. Developing in-service training of various kinds is dealt with in the following two chapters. Some useful resource books for these specific kinds of communication training are worth mentioning here.

Although it is a book primarily directed toward improving teaching, *T.E.T.* (Teacher Effectiveness Training) is a personal favorite in terms of the way it handles communication. Much of the approach suggested for teacher–student interaction is equally valid for teacher–teacher communication. The author of *T.E.T.* is Thomas Gordon, who also wrote *Group Centered Leadership: A Way of Releasing the Creative Power of Groups*.

Another source worth investigating is George Gazda's *Human Relations Development*.

Problem solving is the second focus of in-service training prior to actual circle functioning. Here again, there are some excellent sources of inspiration for such training. Of particular merit is *Conceptual Blockbusting* by James L. Adams. Subtitled *A Pleasurable Guide to Better Problem Solving*, this 133-page paperback provides many exercises and ideas that can be used in groups. It's a good resource for tackling problems of stereotypical thinking.

New Think and *Lateral Thinking: A Step by Step Guide*, works of Edward DeBono, are also excellent books. "Lateral thinking" is DeBono's term for creative thinking that seeks alternatives by restructuring rather than building upon established ideas.

By training in communication and problem solving at the outset, the circle establishes a foundation of knowledge and skills upon which to build solid working relationships. These relationships ensure that the group functions on-target effectively and consistently.

It is essential that this four-step plan be considered carefully and implemented systematically. By doing so, the school leader can be reasonably certain that any quality circle formed will both understand its functions and limitations *and* live within those parameters and act accordingly.

THE ROLE OF THE FACILITATOR

If, as in the example illustrated in Figure 9-2, the facilitator or group leader is to be chosen by the group, it would be a good idea to consider what qualities such a facilitator should possess. Some suggestions are:

- The facilitator should be willing to "go the extra mile" to acquire additional training, put in extra time when needed, and so on. Leadership is often strenuous and time consuming.
- The facilitator should like people and get along well with other staff members. Ideally, he or she is well-liked, even admired, perhaps a natural diplomat.
- The facilitator should be a leader who can keep a group on task, work by an agenda, and relate to all levels of participation.
- The facilitator should be an effective trainer of peer professionals, able not only to lead but to instruct when the need arises.

What, then, does the chosen facilitator actually do? In serving the quality circle in its post-training period—i.e., after completing the four formation steps discussed earlier—the actual work of the quality circle tends to be directed by the facilitator through a series of stages. While these stages will differ from problem to problem and from group to group as problems and styles of problem solving differ, it is possible to identify some major steps. Seven possible stages, arranged in sequential order, are:

1. *Select a problem.* It may be the most significant or pressing of many problems to be taken up, or it may be chosen for other reasons.
2. *Gather facts.* Find out what lies behind the problem. Many a problem is like a patient's fever: only a symptom of something more significant.
3. *Analyze causes.* Having found some underlying cause of the problem, the circle will need to determine its extent, seriousness, and solvability.

4. *Generate a solution.* This is the heart of problem solving. After seeking alternatives, the best potential solution must be chosen.

5. *Implement the solution.* If the circle operates at the decision level of authority, it is up to the group to implement its solution to the problem.

6. *Review.* After implementation, the group should ask, "Did the solution really work?" If not, the problem remains to be re-examined.

7. *Take up the next problem.*

Obviously, this set of stages—a problem-solving cycle—is concerned with only one problem. The quality circle may be considering several problems at once, each at a different stage of solution. For example, a scheduling problem may be in the implementation stage while a problem arising out of a parent's complaining over textbook selection may be in the fact-gathering stage. One of the facilitator's tasks will be to keep the workings of the group from becoming muddled in the complexity inherent in tackling several problems on several levels at the same time.

Finally, it will also fall to the facilitator to be aware of the processing dimension of the quality circle. Is the circle working? How do the members feel about how the circle operates? To this end, the facilitator will want to do some fact gathering of his or her own. Figure 9-4 illustrates a form that may be useful in this respect.

This form, adapted from one suggested by Frank M. Gryna, Jr.[2], will allow the facilitator to collect both negative and positive feedback and to alter group strategies accordingly.

The facilitator's role is an important aspect of the quality circle's success. Who is chosen and how that person functions can well determine the future viability of the group.

MANAGEMENT'S COMMITMENT

Regardless of the level at which a quality circle functions—whether it is a circle of building principals, of teaching staff within a school or department, or of district employees both professional and parapro-

---

[2]Frank M. Gryna, Jr., *Quality Circles: A Team Approach to Problem Solving*, (New York: AMACOM, 1981), p. 64.

ENGLISH DEPARTMENT QUALITY CIRCLE

Facilitator: _____

Meeting on (date): _____

Meeting Topic: _____

Positive Reactions:

Negative Reactions:

Additional Comments:

FIGURE 9-4. Quality Circle Facilitator Feedback Form

fessional—supervisory level management must be committed to making the quality circle concept work.

Keys to this commitment are as follows:

1. A thorough understanding of the quality circle concept, its advantages as a problem-solving forum, and its limitations as a decision-making strategy.

2. Agreement about the value of encouraging staff participation in school management through involvement in a quality circle.

3. Support for the quality circle function: (a) philosophically—i.e., speaking positively about quality circles and actively promoting their formation, and (b) practically—i.e., providing financial support for in-service training, release time, extra pay for extra services for some facilitators, and so on.

4. Willingness to trust staff and to decentralize decision making at some levels of management.

Arch-traditionalists in school management will have initial difficulty with the quality circle concept because it smacks of "administration by committee." As they explore the concept, however, even the most ardent autocrat will come to realize that quality circles must function within a framework acceptable to management and that decision-making control is best exercised not by denying staff members the opportunity to participate in the decision-making process but by recognizing those areas of expertise wherein staff members are the best qualified to make decisions, therefore encouraging them to do so. School leaders who understand that education is a cooperative professional venture will readily recognize that the best decisions are made by those closest to the problem in question.

The teacher's union likewise may have initial problems with the quality circle concept. These problems, too, usually stem from a lack of understanding about the nature, advantages, and limitations of a quality circle. Once understood, the worker participation aspect of a circle will be seen to be valuable and acceptable within the union framework as well.

Any innovation in staff involvement takes time to be integrated within existing management structures and philosophies. Virtually all recent writers on the subject of quality circles have urged the same caution: Go slowly. It takes time and training to build understanding. Acceptance will come with results.

Quality circles are not meant to solve all the problems of modern schooling. But they are a valuable tool in the management repertoire of problem-solving and decision-making strategies. As a means of increasing significant staff involvement in school management, quality circles are well worth investigating.

Developing Effective Staff Training Seminars

10

A great deal has been written in educational journals about the importance of in-service training and how such training can be accomplished efficiently and effectively. In the context of staff involvement, the objective of this chapter and the next is to explore some strategies by which training can be made an element of the integrated approach to school management advocated in this book. That is, how can in-service education both grow out of and further extend staff involvement?

To begin, it is expedient to divide in-service training into two types: seminars and workshops.

A staff seminar is a meeting, or series of meetings, devoted to study and exchange of ideas on one or more educational topics.

The word *seminar* comes from the Latin *seminarium*, meaning "nursery" or "seed plot." Appropriately, the seminar should be an opportunity to cultivate seeds of knowledge shared by the participants.

On the other hand, the term *workshop* takes its definition more directly from the word *work*:

A staff workshop is a meeting, or series of meetings, devoted to the development of a specific educational product.

Again, by bringing staff members together to share ideas and to learn new skills and knowledge, the workshop functions similarly to the seminar as an educational vehicle. The difference between the seminar and the workshop lies in the type of outcome produced by each.

In the seminar, the outcome is primarily personal growth. Knowledge is internalized and strengthens the individual staff member's practices by the building of fresh insights and enhanced experience.

By contrast, in a workshop the outcome is externalized in the form of a specific product or set of products. Individually, it may be a lesson plan that can be used in the staff member's own classroom in the future. Or it may be a new assessment instrument to diagnose student learning needs. Collectively, the staff workshop product may be a new curriculum guide put together by staff members from the same discipline or an interdisciplinary learning strategy developed by staff members from diverse disciplines.

All of this is not to say that a seminar *cannot* produce a specific product. Rather the distinction is that a seminar is a learning opportunity that *may* produce a tangible outcome, while a workshop is a learning opportunity *designed to* produce a tangible outcome.

This distinction—albeit seemingly slight—establishes the groundwork needed to keep on target these two special kinds of staff training as effective modes of in-service education.

Since each of these modes has specific characteristics, it will be necessary to consider them separately. For this reason, seminars are taken up in the remainder of this chapter, and workshops are dealt with in Chapter Eleven.

DEFINING A TOPICAL FOCUS

In developing successful in-service seminars, it is essential that the seminars begin from a topical focus. That is, the direction and content of each seminar must take its impetus from staff-perceived needs.

Adults learn best when they perceive the instruction to be of personal value. When seminar topics focus on what teachers really want to know, seminars are more likely to result in real learning. The focus of any seminar is best derived from the staff members or others who will participate, rather than being decided at the administrative level.

Certainly, there are topics that reappear annually, including classroom discipline, instructional planning, evaluation and grading, and similar broad topics. However, part of the assumption of worth in in-service training is the notion that the instruction/learning that takes place in conjunction with work—i.e., while staff are "in service"—is in part valuable because it can be more current than similar learning in more a formalized setting, such as in the college or university classroom.

The value of determining a topical focus, therefore, comes from exploiting the double meaning of *topical*.

First, the focus of any seminar must be *directed* toward a topic that concerns the staff members who are to participate in the seminar —a subject about which they believe they *need* to know more.

Second, the focus must be topical in the sense that it is "*of the moment*." The best seminars are those that deal with current issues and questions not being examined in other settings. The effective seminar does not attempt to replicate the college classroom. Rather, it breaks fresh ground for contemporary issues.

What do staff members want to learn in a seminar? What do these individuals believe they *need* to know more about? How can these needs and desires be discovered by the school leader charged with developing the in-service experience?

A first step toward answering these questions may well be to fall back on a familiar—but efficient—method of gathering staff input: the staff survey, discussed in Chapter Four. A sample survey to answer these questions is found in Figure 10-1.

Figure 10-1 or a similar survey can be used to find out what topics appeal most to staff members. In the example, the respondents have an opportunity to express both their personal needs as well as those of their department, as they see them. There is the option, too, of building on previously explored topics and of including nonschool/non-department members in the in-service experiences.

This sort of survey can be administered at the start of the school year (as indicated by the date of September 15), or at the close of school the previous spring. A spring survey permits planning to take place during the summer months but may involve some shortcomings. For instance, some staff members may not be "geared up" to think about future in-service options when they are busy winding down the school year. Then, too, needs change. The perceptions of spring may not be valid the next fall. When the spring survey is used, it is a good idea to follow up in the fall with a "check back" sort of survey that seeks to confirm that those ideas expressed once are still current needs and interests.

To the Faculty:

This school year staff members will have several opportunities to participate in in-service seminars and workshops. In order to plan topics of interest to you, please complete the following statements regarding your personal and departmental in-service needs. Return this form to Mrs. Larson by 4:00 P.M., Friday, September 15.

Personal Interests and Needs

1. I want to learn more about _____

2. I could use workshop time to develop _____

3. I might be willing to lead a seminar or workshop to _____

Departmental Interests and Needs

1. Members of my department want to learn more about _____

2. We could use a departmental workshop in order to develop

3. I would be interested in participating in a seminar or workshop led by _____

(NOTE: Feel free to list several items in each space above.)

Other Suggestions

_____

_____

_____

_____

Extended Experiences

Should any topics dealt with last year be reexamined or further developed? If so, which ones? _____

_____

Should any individuals outside the school or department be included in this year's in-service plans? If so, who and why?

_____

_____

_____

FIGURE 10-1. Staff In-service Needs

ACHIEVING PARTICIPATION AND SUPPORT

Simply basing in-service seminars on staff-expressed interests, however, is no guarantee that active participation and support will be achieved. In order to assure these favorable outcomes—and they must be viewed as *outcomes* rather than prerequisites—it will be necessary at the outset to strive for some qualitative characteristics.

These characteristics may be termed incentives or motivators, since their presence will tend to stimulate staff interest in in-service education and generate positive attitudes that result in active participation and support. Some of these motivators are:

1. The in-service seminar should *build self-esteem.* Not only should the seminar engender new learning, but it should give participants opportunities to display their own expertise. Going back to the definition of a seminar as it was presented earlier, " A staff seminar is a meeting . . . to study and exchange ideas . . .''

2. The seminar should *build peer acceptance.* By fostering a setting in which positive human relations are possible, by establishing trust and honest give-and-take of ideas, a seminar should enhance feelings of cohesiveness among staff members.

3. The seminar should *be important in terms of administrative commitment.* With some justification many teachers believe that if in-service work is *important*, it should not be merely an add-on program—i.e., something that staff members are expected to do in their spare time. Providing released time from classes in order to permit staff members to attend school-sponsored in-service seminars is one way of making such programs important, because it demonstrates a time-and-money commitment on the part of the district or school administration.

4. Participation in the seminar should *be rewarded.* Few people engage in structured learning experiences solely for their personal amusement. Since many school systems are committed to continuous learning, often as a requisite for continued employment, in-service seminars should logically carry a reward of points or credits toward fulfilling the district requirement for continuing education. This aspect, again, prevents in-service education from being seen as merely an add-on, and makes it an integral part of the district's professional expectations.

Not long ago, two Pennsylvania State University educators, Fred H. Wood and Steven R. Thompson, zeroed in on several of the current problems concerning in-service education.[1] Among these problems, they identified the following:

- negative attitudes held by staff toward in-service education
- administrators' view of teachers as being opposed to involvement in professional growth
- districtwide focus rather than school- or staff-specific focus in in-service programs

By tailoring in-service seminars to the needs and interests expressed by staff members through the use of research surveys or in other ways, and by building in-service programs that are comfortable and supportive and result in tangible rewards, school leaders can avoid these problems.

Wood and Thompson frame similar suggestions in terms of:

- increasing participant control over the learning situation
- focusing on tasks that are viewed as "real" and "important"
- providing alternative programs to suit individual needs
- including practice and simulation
- encouraging small groups and the exchange of ideas
- reducing external judgments—e.g., from administrators—while encouraging peer feedback.

CHOOSING LOGICAL SEQUENCES

There are several reasonable steps, or stages, that should be taken to create a successful educational seminar. Before proceeding to the actual seminar sequence, however, there are some preliminary considerations. Paramount among these is the selection of a seminar leader. Often, it falls to the building principal to serve as the in-service leader, and equally as often the principal is not an expert in the seminar's subject field. This circumstance can be an advantage or a disadvantage, depending upon the attitude of the principal.

Whenever possible, the seminar leader should be someone who is qualified, experienced, and enthusiastic about the seminar topic. The

---

[1]Fred H. Wood and Steven R. Thompson, "Guidelines for Better Staff Development," *Educational Leadership*, February 1980, pp. 374–378.

district's curriculum director, another faculty member, or an individual from the community may serve. Likewise, instructors from local colleges may be interested in leading in-service seminars. Failing all of these possibilities, it is still possible for the principal or some other "nonexpert" to conduct a seminar successfully *if* a "learning together" attitude is adopted.

"Learning together" means that the seminar leader exercises management and leadership skills to establish the seminar and move the learning experience through its various stages, but he or she does not assume the role of a subject expert. While at first glance this approach may seem fraught with problems, surprisingly it often proves to be quite advantageous. For example, it offers the principal a chance to get close to staff members, to be seen in a different light—a view that often produces increased mutual understanding. Also, it offers an opportunity for staff and administration to gain common understandings of subject matter, an action that may result in better curriculum development in the future.

Given the expert or the nonexpert as seminar leader, it is possible to continue on a course suitable for either. Some other preliminary considerations:

Size: Since seminars are designed to produce dialog, in most instances it will be best to limit the group size to no more than twenty. An exception might be granted where there are several seminar leaders, and large groups can be separated into several smaller groups for discussions.

Time: As noted earlier, seminars should be conducted during regular working hours. Staff should not be expected to give up personal time without pay for school-sponsored in-service work.

Place: Setting is important enough to be considered separately; therefore, it is taken up in another section.

With these preliminaries under control, what are the stages that provide a logical sequence for a seminar?

STAGE ONE—Goal-Setting

Establishing a topic does not establish a goal. It is important to take any given topic and to ask pertinent questions:

- What is it about this topic that staff want to learn?
- Of the areas encompassed by the topic, which are germane to our specific needs?

By focusing on specific goals or objectives, the seminar leader will avoid diffusion—that is, everyone mentally going off in all directions with the result that little learning is actually accomplished.

By setting goals with the group fully participating, the seminar leader not only establishes a positive direction in which to lead the group learning experience, but he or she also sets up criteria by which the learning experience can be evaluated.

STAGE TWO—Individual Learning

STAGE THREE—Group Learning

These stages are often sequential, but it is equally true that the stages—in a two-step cycle—repeat many times in the typical seminar.

In the first instance, individual learners are exposed to new ideas that come from the expert leader or from various readings, films, research, and so on. The individual then takes these learning experiences and integrates them with existing knowledge.

In Stage Three, the individual learners interact with one another to share knowledge and insights, resulting in common understanding and group learning.

Depending upon the topic, the goals, and the leader's strategies, the repetition of Stage Two–Stage Three cycles may occur many times, resulting in significant personal learning on the part of individual staff participants as well as building a body of common knowledge about the seminar subject.

STAGE FOUR—Closure and Evaluation

The final stage of any seminar is the act of closure. Again, it may be helpful to suggest some questions:

- What will be done with the new knowledge?
- How will the common understandings be used and strengthened beyond the seminar?

Along with these closure questions, some consideration should be given to the evaluation of the seminar:

- Were the goals of the seminar reached?
- How can future seminars be improved, based on the experience of this seminar?

(Evaluating and refining the seminar will be discussed in detail in a later section.)

Figure 10-2 illustrates the four-stage sequence graphically.

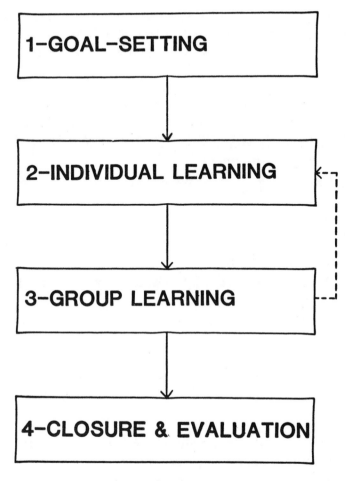

FIGURE 10-2

By building this logical sequence—or a relevant adaptation—the seminar leader can be assured that both personal and group learning will take place and that specific goals will be reached.

ATTENTION TO EDUCATIONAL MATERIALS

Unlike college coursework, where lengthy reading assignments and outside research appropriately augment classroom instruction, the in-service seminar's needs are much simpler and more direct.

Educational materials for in-service seminars should be matched to the specific objective(s) of the seminar. They should be limited to those materials that are concise and ready-to-use; and they should be used on the spot rather than assigned as outside readings.

Figure 10-3 is a checklist of characteristics for in-service seminar materials.

_____ Does the reading pertain directly to the seminar?

_____ Can the material be read in less than ten minutes? (i.e., during the seminar)

_____ Are visual materials (films, filmstrips, etc.) brief and to-the-point?

_____ Do the materials use real situations as examples?

_____ Do the materials contain concrete examples—positive-negative, pro–con?

_____ Do the materials allow the leader to integrate written and visual material with the discussions?

_____ Are the materials clear?

FIGURE 10-3. Checklist for Seminar Materials

A few words are necessary regarding the last question in Figure 10-3: "Are the materials clear?" Educators have a noticeable penchant for producing copies of articles, manuscripts, and so on that defy readability. Doubtless there are many seminar participants who have spent ten minutes just attempting to discern which words those fuzzy shapes on the page constituted, let alone finding any meaning that might be hidden in the text. Copies of copies of copies simply won't do the job.

A clear text is essential. If it is to be a spirit copy (i.e., Ditto), the original should be a newly typed master. Anything less runs the risk of producing merely illegible fuzz.

Seminar leaders can help out the readability process, too, by taking that clear copy and highlighting important points with underlining, arrows, asterisks, and similar devices that visually draw attention. The same technique can be used for overhead transparency presentations.

A word of caution: Be aware of copyright restrictions. The copyright laws occasionally change, and it is a good idea to find out the latest restrictions before using materials in an illegal way. Rather than copying published materials, look for reprint services and specialized publications to meet the seminar's material requirements.

FINDING THE BEST SETTING

The setting for an educational seminar is a factor too often given very little consideration. Yet, it is often where we work that influences how, and *how well*, we work.

For an in-service seminar, it is usually a good idea to place the seminar in a setting apart from the normal school setting. When seminars are held in the school where teacher participants normally teach, there is always the temptation of interruptions and intrusions of the "usual" (daily teaching duties) into the "special" (the seminar). The seminar should be special. To be optimally successful, it should be a transition from work or teaching to learning. For this reason alone, it is a good idea to secure a seminar location apart from the normal workplace.

At the same time, the seminar is a part of the work world; therefore, the location should be businesslike. The "training resort" popular in the business world would be of questionable value. More preferable would be a conference room at the local college or technical institute; a public room at a bank; a private room in a restaurant; the school district's central administrative facility in larger school systems; or a local lodge hall. The possibilities vary from community to community.

Some general characteristics that may serve as appropriate guidelines are:

1. Find a room away from the normal work area.
2. Choose a facility that has ample space for the seminar group but that is not overlarge.
3. Pick a well-lit, well-ventilated, and businesslike room.
4. Make sure the room has adequate table space. (A large conference table is ideal for groups up to ten persons. More than that number calls for several separate tables.)
5. Ascertain the availability of and placement of electrical outlets for film projectors, tape players, and other powered aids.
6. Find a location that is easily accessible for participants and has ample parking.

In summary, giving attention to selecting the best possible facility will enhance the seminar effort. While a superb conference room cannot strengthen a weak seminar, it is certainly true that a cramped, uncomfortable meeting place can weaken even the best seminar.

EVALUATING AND REFINING THE SEMINAR

An integral part of any seminar should be evaluation. Even in cases where the particular seminar is a one-time experience, the successes and failures of the in-service work improve future seminars on other topics.

In particular, seminar leaders will want to know whether the objectives established in Stage One have been accomplished. One way to do this in Stage Four of the seminar is to ask participants to rate the accomplishment of each objective.

Figure 10-4 shows one way of structuring the rating.

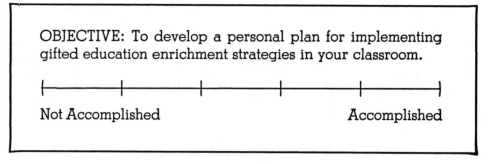

FIGURE 10-4. Sliding Scale Rating

In this figure, the respondent is asked to rate the degree to which the objective was accomplished. This scale is marked off in five sections. Some raters prefer scales from 0–8, 1–10, or other variations. The sections allow the seminar leader to convert the ratings into numerical figures for easier comparison and analysis.

In addition to rating the objectives, participants may be asked to evaluate the timing of the seminar (e.g., how it fits into their activities in the classroom, how it jibes with overall district in-service objectives), the setting, the leader's activities, the quality of the readings and visuals, and other pertinent aspects of the in-service experience.

It is particularly useful to have a couple of open-ended questions that highlight the experience. These questions can be as simple as:

What was the most valuable thing you learned in this seminar?

What was the least valuable thing you learned in this seminar?

Alternatives:

Which seminar activity benefited you the most?

Which learning segment would you most want another colleague to experience?

Which activity was least valuable?

Would you eliminate any particular learning segment from future seminars, and why?

By gaining as much input as possible about the seminar experience from the participants, the seminar leader can effectively remove or strengthen weak aspects of the in-service work while retaining those segments or activities that are strong.

TEN GUIDELINES TO SUCCESSFUL IN-SERVICE TRAINING

Along with the group's evaluation of the seminar, what about the leader's own self-evaluation? Here are ten guidelines in the form of questions the seminar leader should ask him- or herself:

1. Did I begin with a topic that was identified as valuable in the eyes of the participants and lead the group in planning *specific objectives* for the in-service seminar?

2. Did I use participant's ideas to build self-esteem and peer recognition as positive reinforcements for all members of the seminar group?

3. Did I demonstrate an administrative commitment to the importance of the in-service seminar?

4. Did I encourage the exchange of ideas by limiting my own external judgments?

5. Did I arrange for a time and place for the seminar that demonstrated concern for the group's comfort?

6. Did I conduct the seminar in an orderly, step-by-step fashion, so that ideas and discussions followed one another logically and easily?

7. Did I select materials that were concise, clear, and pertinent?

8. Did I relate new information to actual work experiences?

9. Did I find out how the participants felt about the in-service seminar in order to make appropriate changes?

10. Did I take time to reflect on my own role and to plan for personal changes as needed?

By using these questions, the seminar leader can assess the strengths and weaknesses of the in-service experience and his or her role in it. No seminar is perfect the first time; few are perfect the hundredth. Through introspection and observation, however, each seminar can be more effective than the last, regardless of the specific topic of the in-service experience.

Planning Workshops
That Work

11

AS identified in Chapter Ten, a staff workshop is "a meeting, or series of meetings, devoted to the development of a specific educational product." The key word here is *product*. Unlike the seminar, where the results tend to be internalized new knowledge and new understandings, the outcome of a workshop should be some form of educational product. This product may be a teaching plan for an individual, a group instructional approach, a set of learning materials, a new curriculum guide, or perhaps merely a new way of working together. The word *product* should connote tangibility and substance. Whether or not the product is "on paper" is a secondary consideration.

What, then, are the characteristics of a staff workshop?

EXPLORING WORKSHOP CHARACTERISTICS

One way to begin would be to define *tangibility* more closely.

A distinguishing characteristic of the workshop is the way in which participants work together toward the in-service goals. Let's assume that a goal of a particular workshop is to develop increased staff harmony. To reach this goal, the group is led through a series of interpersonal relations activities by a competent, experienced leader. The result of this series of workshop activities in terms of increasing positive staff interaction can be documented, even though the group itself does not produce anything "on paper." Nonetheless, this documentable result is *tangible*; it is a product of substance.

Two characteristics of a workshop are:

1. A workshop is product-oriented.
2. A workshop is group-oriented.

But there is yet a third characteristic, one that distinguishes the staff workshop from its counterparts in the business world—that is, the educational staff workshop is to some degree devoted to the task of learning. Staff participants in most in-service workshops are expected not only to reach group goals and produce tangible results, but to learn new skills and acquire new knowledge by their participation in the workshop. Thus, another characteristic:

3. A workshop is education-oriented.

To make a finer distinction between the seminar and workshop form of in-service education, it should be pointed out that a staff seminar is generally oriented toward internalized learning rather than production of some external product, thus making it more characteristically individual-oriented—even though the setting of the seminar is a group.

These three workshop characteristics, or orientations, require that a workshop be thought of somewhat differently than a staff seminar and, consequently, designed with different considerations in mind.

By exploring these new considerations, it is possible to create staff workshops that work—workshops that focus on groups which develop *real* products and accomplish *real* learning.

SETTING REAL AND REACHABLE GOALS

It is especially important to the success of any workshop that tangible, reachable goals be established by the group. Notice here that there are three important aspects to this goal-setting task:

First, established goals must reflect the down-to-earth quality of a *work*shop. That is, the goals must be directed toward a tangible end.

Second, the goals must be realistic in the sense that they are within the participants' capabilities. By this definition, such goals are *reachable*—that is, they are reasonably capable of being achieved by the group.

Third, the goals must be defined and established *by the group*. Externally imposed goals will not tend to produce results as successfully as internally generated ones. This is not to say, however, that a group cannot be directed. There can certainly be an administrative direction and general criteria for accomplishment. But the current goals are better generated by the group within the broader administrative guidelines. The group's self-determination is a factor that helps to mold the group into a working unit by stimulating ownership of the group goals and participation in the goal achievement.

In setting effective goals, the concept of *consensus* is worth taking a moment to explore. Because we live in a democratic society, we sometimes tend to believe that some form of voting is the best way to establish rules, guidelines, procedures, goals, and so on. Unfortunately, in the democratic procedure there tends to be a winning side and one or more losing sides. Where group work is concerned, this winner –loser split is sometimes more likely to produce either active or passive discord and resistance. The win–lose dichotomy weakens group cohesiveness. Majority rule works reasonably well for society at large, but for workshop groups another alternative is needed.

Consensus provides that alternative in group decision making. A brief definition is:

> *Consensus means general agreement or accord based on collective opinion.*

The word *consensus* takes its form from the Latin root of *consent*, which is *consentire*, meaning "to feel together"—in other words, "to agree."

While consensus would be impossible as a societal decision-making form, it is ideal for the smaller world of the workshop group because it allows every participant to be a winner. A group functioning through consensus is one in which each member has agreed to the goals, procedures, and responsibilities of the group. This common agreement forms a bond of task commitment that is not as likely to be present in groups where decisions are made "democratically" with the will of the majority being imposed on the minority. The consensus-run group leader will find the most frequently asked question is: "Do we all agree to this?"

Is consensus easier to use? No. Sometimes it takes considerable time to iron out differences of viewpoint and to reach general agreement within a group. (It is much easier to say, "Let's just vote on it!" which immediately cuts out some members of the group.)

Is consensus more effective? Yes. When everyone agrees, the group runs smoother. Everyone has a stake in the workshop's outcomes and individual members are more likely to work directly toward making the workshop work.

DISCOVERING WORKER SKILLS/DEFINING WORKER ROLES

Part of any goal-setting process should be the discovery of those methods or techniques that may be effective in reaching goals. Inherent in any method or technique is a body of skills. These skills may be denoted in a variety of ways, as follows:

Procedural Skills

Organization
Forecasting
Planning
Evaluating

Technical Skills

Research
Observation
Instruction
Writing
Illustrating

Clerical Skills

Typing
Shorthand
Filing
Printing (reproduction)

These skills are those most frequently called upon by workshop groups, but there are others that may be needed as well. For instance, a science workshop might break down the necessary skills into subject specialties, such as biology, botany, chemistry, physics, and so forth. Likewise, a group working with a home economics curriculum project might prefer to divide their skills among such headings as cooking, sewing, weaving, and the like.

In any case, among the first tasks of the workshop group will be the defining of the types of skills that will be needed to reach the group's goals. Having once completed this definition process, it will then be necessary to survey the group to find out which individuals can best handle the individual skill areas.

In many instances, this survey process can be handled informally, particularly if the members of the group know one another reasonably well. In other cases, where participants have been brought together for a workshop without being acquainted previously, it can be helpful to use a more direct survey strategy, such as listing the necessary skills areas and simply asking participants to rate their own interests and skills.

Figure 11-1 shows how one such survey might be filled out by a workshop participant.

SEWING CURRICULUM WORKSHOP

ELLENTOWN JUNIOR HIGH SCHOOL

Workshop Participant: Please rate your interest and skill in the following areas. Use this system:

3 – High   2 – Moderate   1 – Low

Needed Skills:	*Interest*	*Skill*
Library research	1	1
Personal sewing	3	3
Curriculum development	3	2
Demonstration sewing	3	3
Typing	1	2
Making bulletin boards	2	1
Public speaking	1	1

Your name: _Grace Ames_

FIGURE 11-1

These surveys are subsequently collected by the workshop leader who makes a master list which is announced and discussed. Final role assignments should be posted somewhere on the workshop site, so that all participants know who is supposed to do what.

It may be useful to review Part One of this book, since many of the organizational strategies found there can be put to excellent use in the context of a workshop. Larger workshops in particular will benefit from being able to utilize the same types of grouping strategies outlined for committees. Encouraging small groups to work and learn within the larger workshop body can be beneficial both for the individuals and for the whole group.

TIME, SPACE, AND MATERIAL REQUIREMENTS

In many instances, a workshop may require little that is different in terms of time, space, and materials from those required by the seminar, as discussed in the previous chapter. However, the *work* nature of a workshop sometimes dictates that additional space be provided, that additional time be allotted, and that a variety of materials be procured for use by the group.

The wise group leader will consider these requirements as much as possible in advance of the workshop session(s). In initial planning for most workshops, it is probable that some gauge of time can be determined, either based on similar workshops in the same school or school district or by checking with contemporaries in other nearby communities regarding their experiences. However, the real key to success in workshop planning is *flexibility*. Since it is important to allow participants a measure of latitude regarding the course of the workshop, it will be necessary to remain flexible regarding the amount of time to be devoted to workshop activities.

The same considerations can be applied to space and materials. Prior experience will be an invaluable guide, but flexibility is by far the best characteristic that can be applied to workshop leadership. Keep in mind that an underlying assumption and, consequently, an underlying goal is that groups will function most competently when allowed a greater degree of self-determination. Leadership in this context guides without unduly constraining, which results in maximum involvement and participation.

Here are some guidelines for the workshop leader to consider in maintaining that "delicate balance" between constraint and leadership —guidelines that will aid in maintaining *flexibility*:

1. Find out the needs of the group as early in the workshop process as possible. If goals can be established early, it will be easier to plan effectively for the time, space, and material requirements.

2. Communicate time and location information clearly. Use more than one method of communication—e.g., the school bulletin *and* a personal note, or a telephone call *and* a posted announcement. Make sure that participants know when and where they are to meet.

3. Maintain an ongoing list of needed materials, and allow participants to add items and suggestions as they think of them. Many times we sit down to make a list only to discover later that several items were not considered. An ongoing list helps to avoid spur-of-the-moment omissions.

4. Plan some material alternatives ahead of time. For instance, will the group need an overhead projector? Who knows? Check out one anyway, just in case. Several items can be handled in this "just in case" fashion; for example: pencils and paper, chalkboards, projectors, typewriters, and masking tape. It is better to have to return a few unused items to the supply room than to have to send out for such items while the workshop group waits.

Flexibility means to be open to alternatives—and to know what those alternatives are. Workshop leaders who take time to analyze their potential needs ahead of time will be better able to cope with unexpected needs. They will be able to be flexible.

MEETING AS A FUNCTION OF WORKING

While flexibility will be an asset in any case, advanced planning may relieve some of the potential for problems that can demand flexibility.

Typically, educational workshops tend to be planned by administrators for their staff, or by some staff members for other staff members. In other words, those individuals who will actually participate in the workshop often are not involved in its planning.

The approach advocated in this chapter is designed basically to counteract the negatives generated by this external planning. That is, when a workshop is broadly conceived by other than the participants, it should be within the purview of those participants to direct the internal workings of the workshop—i.e., goal-setting, activity planning, and so on. These internal controls build the vital self-determination needed to engender feelings of ownership, which in turn produce effective results.

This approach, however, is remedial in character. Advanced planning should be considered an integral part of the workshop itself. This means that future workshop participants should be the ones to plan their own workshop—rather than administrators or other staff members.

This suggestion can appropriately be characterized by recognizing *meeting* as a function of *working*. The sequence of events might progress in this way:

First, a decision is made to conduct a workshop. On what grounds is this decision made? Chapter Four suggested several types of information-gathering techniques that might be used to discover staff needs in areas of in-service work. So, the decision to conduct a workshop is appropriately an administrative one.

At this point, the administration can announce a broadly based workshop opportunity as an initial effort to recruit participants. At the same time, the administration communicates that those staff members interested in pursuing the workshop opportunity will have the chance to design the workshop to suit their needs, rather than to simply participate in an administratively pre-programmed in-service seminar.

Second, a workshop group is formed to design the workshop experience. *This is the meeting.*

This advanced planning meeting is the place where future participants determine the content and direction of the workshop.

Then, at some later time, the actual workshop is held. Those who planned the workshop are the participants.

What ramifications does this suggestion hold? One consequence is that "normal" workshop scheduling must be rethought to accommodate the meeting element. It means that instead of scheduling, say, a five-day block of workshop time, a one-day planning session might be held one week, with the actual workshop being a four-day session two or three weeks later.

An advantage of this schedule is that the lead time—between the meeting and the workshop—gives the workshop leader the opportunity to set up facilities and materials more efficiently. The lead time *provides* flexibility, whereas lack of it *demands* flexibility. This is a significant difference.

Still another factor in favor of the meeting for advance planning is that it frees participants to consider working options that might not otherwise be considered. More alternatives are likely to be available on two or three weeks' notice (i.e., when planning is done that amount of time in advance) than would be available on a day's notice (i.e., when planning is done on the first day of a five-day workshop session).

All things considered, it will pay fine dividends if school leaders will consider structuring workshop in-services differently than they are presently structured by most school districts.

The key factors are:

- Advanced planning to provide lead time, so that the workshop can run as smoothly as possible.
- Advanced planning *by workshop participants* to ensure that individual needs are met and that appropriate feelings of ownership are engendered.

DEVELOPING APPROPRIATE OWNERSHIP

The concept of ownership was defined as a "belief that a problem or task is possessed and controlled by an individual or group." It is reasonable to reiterate here the importance of this concept.

In adult education particularly, the recognition of ownership's importance to working and learning is vital to success. Researchers Wood and Thompson, cited earlier, suggest several influential factors in the effectiveness of staff in-service education[1]:

- Adults need to view goals as realistic and important.
- Adults need to view learning as either personally or professionally relevant
- Adults need to see results—a tangible product.
- Adults need experiences that are individualized and self-directed.
- Adult motivation comes from a desire to be involved as well as a desire to be recognized.
- Adults need educational opportunities that are ego-supportive and that do not appear as attacks on competence.
- Adults need leadership that emphasizes respect, trust, and concern.
- Adults need to be the originators of their own learning.

These factors reinforce the idea that it is important to involve staff members thoroughly in their in-service education. These factors, in fact, are the embodiment of "ownership."

---

[1]Fred H. Wood and Steven R. Thompson, "Guidelines for Better Staff Development," *Educational Leadership*, February 1980, p. 376.

COMPLETION, SUCCESS, REWARD, FOLLOW-UP

While significant involvement and self-determination may have their own reward, there is still a need for external recognition from peers and administrators.

Other chapters of this book have dealt with evaluation and follow-up, so it is not necessary to belabor those points here. Suffice it to say, success is seldom measured immediately after any given experience. An in-service workshop is no exception. The product created in the workshop will need to be tried and proven. Steps must be taken to ensure some form of follow-up. Is the new curriculum guide actually being used? Did the instructional technique developed by the group prove to be more effective than previous methods? These and similar questions will ultimately prove the success (or failure) of the workshop.

Dear Miss Ames:

This letter is written to express my appreciation for your contributions to this school. Your efforts in developing the new sewing curriculum for grades 7 and 8 helped to bring about a much-needed change, one that will surely bring many benefits to our future students.

The manner in which the workshop's new curriculum guide was presented to the board of education resulted in a fine news article in the local newspaper. This is the sort of "good press" our school needs. You are t be congratulated on your role in this respect also.

Please be advised that a copy of this letter will be placed in your personnel file. Again, my personal thanks are extended to you for your excellent work.

Yours sincerely,

Richard A. Maren

Richard A. Maren
Principal

FIGURE 11-2

But questions of ultimate success aside, there is a need to reward participants for their efforts, to thank them publicly for their time, involvement, and personal concern.

Two important characteristics that this recognition should exhibit are:

1. *The reward should be tangible.* A certificate of accomplishment or a letter of appreciation is usually significant. Some school districts award placques or pins. Others provide the participants with a dinner at which their accomplishments are lauded. It is perhaps wisest to suit the reward to the accomplishment; small accomplishments merit perhaps only a token reward, while large accomplishments merit substantial reward. School and district experience and policy will usually dictate appropriate responses.

Figure 11-2 illustrates how a letter of appreciation might be written.

Bound in a presentation folder and written on the school's official stationery, the letter of appreciation is a worthy reward for service rendered. Similarly, a certificate—perhaps a Distinguished Service Award—can be presented in a formal manner, which enhances the prestige and pride felt by the recipient.

2. *The award should be made publicly.* Whether it is done at a routine meeting or on some special occasion, any reward for service should be presented publicly. This act conveys greater importance on both the act that earned the reward and on the reward recipient.

A further step should be taken to broaden that public beyond the school group. Peer recognition is most important, but since education is a public business, public recognition in the community sense is also important. This community recognition can be accomplished through radio and newspaper press releases in many instances. Reward presentations at PTA meetings and other "open house" kinds of affairs also accomplish this end.

Robert Browning said, "A minute's success pays the failure of years." While staff members have by no means suffered the "failure of years," nevertheless many debts are paid by a moment in the public sun. Administrators who reward will themselves reap the rewards of a staff that is motivated and that feels that the school and its problems and successes are theirs to share.

Beyond Staff Involvement: Exploring the Concept of Shared Governance

12

SO far this book has concentrated on strategies for developing *staff* involvement in school management. But what about the other publics of the school: the parents and the community at large? Is it possible for them to share in school management? Is their involvement desirable?

In the past ten years or so, educators increasingly have found it necessary to ask these questions. The nation's large school districts, faced by pressures to reform traditional school structures and to become more accountable, have in many instances turned to decentralization as a means of enhancing school-community relations and of garnering greater community input.

COMMUNITY CONTROL VERSUS COMMUNITY PARTICIPATION

A nationwide 1980 survey of school systems with 50,000 or more students revealed that approximately 64 percent of the nation's large school systems had adopted some form of decentralized governance.[1]

With decentralization, however, concerns have also arisen regarding the management of the decentralized units. At the heart of these concerns is the question of community control versus community participation.

Allan C. Ornstein, writing in *Principal*, reports that school officials have usually been reluctant to give over substantial control of schools to community groups. Indeed, some large districts—Ornstein cites Los Angeles, Philadelphia, and Portland—have taken the position that community control is likely to be more harmful than helpful.[2]

Community *participation* is another story altogether. School officials in both large and small school systems have seen the benefits of involving the community in the school management function. With the possible exception of personnel matters, community members undertaking advisory roles in school management have been welcomed, and their input has been both appreciated and, more important, used by school officials.

THE QUESTION OF AUTHORITY

Much of the conflict between community control and community participation devolves to the level of authority at which the community group may be allowed to operate—or, perhaps, the level of authority at which the community group is content to operate. With rare exceptions, it is the school administration which has ultimate control over whether a community group functions at a higher or lower level of authority. (The term *school administration*, in this instance, includes the board of education as well as the topline administrators, notably the superintendent and principals.)

Community groups, too, must understand and accept the level of authority at which they function. Chapter Eight's information about staff advisory boards will apply equally well to community advisory groups. The accent is on the word *advisory*, since it is at the advisory level that community groups are likely to be seen in the most positive light by educators, both administrators and teachers.

It seems useful to repeat here the "Six Steps to a Successful Ad-

---

[1] Allan C. Ornstein, "Decentralized School Governance: Is It Working?" *Principal*, November 1981, pp. 24–27.

[2] *Ibid.*

visory Board'' that appeared in Chapter Eight, but with special emphasis on the *community* advisory group.

1. *Clearly define the goals and purposes of the advisory board.*
   The management of schools is a specialized task, complex
   even when taken on by trained educators. School officials
   must make a special effort to ensure that community members
   understand basic educational goals and how the advisory
   group's own goals fit into the overall school picture.

2. *Be certain that the group understands its level of authority is
   the recommendation level.* Just as time must be spent
   educating staff about authority, so must time be given over to
   in-service training for community groups. This is especially
   true because community members often are not educators and
   thus do not have the background in educational management
   that school people have. Part of the success of the advisory
   group will depend on developing a common base of understanding upon which to build.

3. *Develop a representative structure.* As with the staff advisory
   board, every effort should be expended to ensure a broad constituency. This is an important factor to consider in most communities but especially in those of diverse ethnic, racial,
   social, and religious composition.

4. *Help the advisory board build appropriate skills.* Build upon
   the common foundation, mentioned in Step 2 above, by providing opportunities for community members to learn more
   about schools and their management. Of special interest
   should be group work and problem-solving skill development.
   In-service efforts in these areas will be essential.

5. *Build trust by recognizing the board's value.* Use community
   input whenever possible. When advisory group ideas are on-
   target, demonstrate positive reinforcement by putting their
   work into action and commending appropriate groups and individual members.

6. *As the need arises, extend the board beyond its original boun-
   daries.* Use success as a springboard by reinforcing appropriate
   levels of involvement, expanding community input options,
   and enhancing community participation.

SOME DOCUMENTED SUCCESSES

What would you say to some of these successes that have come through community involvement in school governance?

- standardized test scores that have risen above the national norms
- schools that have been closed without a community uproar
- teachers and administrators that are allied on most issues
- a business community that gets involved in the schools' operations
- an immigration of more than seven hundred students from area school systems
- vandalism that has decreased

Sounds too good to be true? Not according to Jerome Cramer's report in *The Executive Educator*.[3]

According to Cramer, these are only some of the positive results achieved by M. Donald Thomas, superintendent of schools in Salt Lake City and one of the leading proponents of shared governance.

Thomas's approach to community involvement led him to develop two community councils at every school in the system. In doing so, he shifted decision-making authority from the principals and vested the running of the schools in the hands of the councils. The two groups—the School Improvement Council and the School Community Council—are composed of teachers, the principal, parents, local citizens, and other personnel. The groups set goals, establish schedules, and decide on matters of curriculum and personnel.

Initial resistance to the shared governance concept is reported to be a thing of the past. Morale is high and teachers and administrators alike would now be reluctant to return to the management style of the past. Thomas has developed a community involvement approach that seems to work well in Salt Lake City. Clearly, much of that approach allows community input to advance beyond mere participation into the area of community control—that is, the level of authority at which the community groups work sometimes exceeds *recommendation*. The success of this endeavor has been Thomas's extensive efforts to

---

[3]Jerome Cramer, "M. Donald Thomas," *The Executive Educator*, February 1983, pp. 13–15.

educate the community about how to become effectively involved in their schools.

In nearly a decade, Thomas has been able to see many of his ideas put into effect in other school systems as well. Among his satellites are Santa Clara, California; Dalton, Georgia; Tulsa, Oklahoma; and Jackson, Mississippi.[4]

SHARED GOVERNANCE IN JACKSON, MISSISSIPPI

The schools in Jackson, Mississippi, use the slogan "Shared Governance: Together We Can Make It Work," and publish a pamphlet entitled *Guidelines for Implementation of Shared Governance* that would serve as a handy resource for any school district contemplating the move to shared governance as a management strategy.

Among the stated goals of shared governance as practiced in Jackson are these:

- enhancing student development
- promoting staff unity
- improving employee morale
- developing a closer school-home relationship
- establishing an atmosphere for creative problem solving
- promoting openness, honesty, and trust
- creating a sense of ownership

Several of the goals relate directly to the decision-making process, such as:

- involving more people in the decision-making process
- promoting sharing in decision making and the responsibility for carrying out decisions
- gaining wider support for decisions
- improving implementation of decisions[5]

Guidelines for Implementation of Shared Governance includes committee work recommendations—i.e., committee composition,

---

[4]*Ibid.*

[5]*Guidelines for Implementation of Shared Governance.* Jackson, Mississippi: Jackson Municipal Separate School District, 1981.

size, responsibilities—and guides to liaison local committees and the central administration. Appendix A of the pamphlet also provides the conceptual framework for in-service training in shared governance.

In all, the Jackson school system's guidelines are well worth investigating by any district thinking about the use of shared governance.

TREADING A THIN LINE

It should be clear from even this brief examination of shared governance that school districts which implement this form of management are treading a thin line between community participation and community control. Therefore, it cannot be overemphasized that a firm understanding of authority—and all its ramifications—is essential.

As stated in the Preface, involvement in the management process (either by staff or by the community at large) does not imply any particular level of authority on the part of the participants. Of course, one outcome of involvement (again, staff or community) may well be that decisions about administrative matters are made by committees rather than administrators. This is indeed participatory management or management by committee. But this outcome is neither essential nor inescapable, and many educators would say that it is not even desirable. The role of school leaders today is to discover how they and their publics can work together to accomplish common goals.

While authority is an extremely important consideration in school management, it should not be allowed to become the central issue. Instead, the central issue should be effective utilization of talent. In the context of staff involvement or community participation, it is those individual talents that can contribute meaningfully to school management that are sought. Those talents will help to achieve the goals so aptly stated by the Jackson schools' publication.

Degrees of participation will differ from district to district. In treading that thin line, some will come closer to community control than others, but the important thing will be for school leaders to recognize the aspirations and the limitations of their staffs and communities. Staff involvement in particular is probably most effective when it grows out of the work process rather than being imposed on that process. This is not to say, of course, that school leaders should merely wait for something to happen in the area of staff participation.

To be effective in staff involvement and community participation, school leaders will need to shrug off old styles of management much as one might shake off an old coat which, although familiar and still reasonably comfortable, no longer affords sufficient protection from the elements. Likewise, there will be staff members who will be asked to accept an unaccustomed and initially uncomfortable role in new areas of concern. All who endeavor to become involved in new management strategies will be required to adopt broader viewpoints and more open stances toward educational and administrative questions. But, to paraphrase Jackson's slogan: Together, staff and administration can make it work. It is the conviction that effective management is aided by meaningfully involving staff which holds promise for the future of American schools.

APPENDICES

- A Short Glossary of Pertinent Terms
- An Easy Guide to Proper Meeting Procedures
- Selected Resources

A Short Glossary
of Pertinent Terms

Appendix A

THIS Appendix provides a ready reference for the major concepts covered in this book. The terms are arranged in alphabetical order and a brief definition of the term as it is used in the context of *How to Build Staff Involvement in School Management* is given.

Action flow chart. Flow chart incorporating both the pattern, or flow, of activity, along with time and responsibility notations.

Advisory board. Faculty committee formed to review school matters and to recommend (i.e., *to advise*) appropriate action to the board's supervisor. This concept is often extended to include community members as part of the advisory board.

Affective communication. Interaction that deals with impressions, feelings, and emotions, as well as with facts.

Authority. Degree to which group conclusions influence or direct management decision making. See *levels of authority.*

Bar graph. Illustration showing the relationship among two or more facts of the same nature. Three main types of bar graphs are vertical, horizontal, and floating.

Brainstorming. Group technique for producing ideas on one or several topics. Ideally, ideas are generated nonjudgmentally, with consideration of an idea's feasibility, practicality, and so on, taking place after the brainstorming process has been completed.

Circular model. Group organizational structure suitable for single-dimensional tasks performed by a small number of persons. See also *linear model* and *modular model.*

Closure. Sense of reaching an appropriate end point or conclusion.

Committee. Group of individuals charged with the responsibility of considering and reporting on specific matters relevant to school programs and/or procedures.

Consensus. General agreement or accord based on collective opinion.

Control. Group's ability or license to direct its own work, such as determining subgoals and work processes.

Creative leadership. Emphasis on openness to new ideas as a function of leadership which transcends traditional definitions of leadership modes or styles—e.g., autocratic, democratic, laissez-faire.

Cut-and-count tabulation. Method by which survey responses are cut apart and counted separately in order to speed hand tabulation.

Decision (level of authority). Highest level of authority; group conclusions are formed as management decisions. See *levels of authority.*

Delegating. Taking a large task and dividing it into workable bits, each one to be accomplished by an individual whose skills and interests suit the needs of the specific job.

Facilities review committee. Advisory board focused on buildings and grounds matters. See also *advisory board.*

Flow chart. Diagram showing the pattern, or flow, of activity within an organization. See also *action flow chart.*

Idea killers. Words or expressions that tend to stop the production of ideas, especially during brainstorming activities. Example: "We did it before."

Information (level of authority). Lowest level of authority; group conclusions provide basic input for external (nongroup) decision making. See *levels of authority.*

Leader. One who directs, coordinates, and/or facilitates the work of others.

Levels of authority. Degrees to which group conclusions influence or direct management decision making. The three levels of authority are *information, recommendation,* and *decision.* See individual level definitions.

Linear model. Group organizational structure using sequentially arranged subgoals that lead toward the main goal. See *linked teams.* See also *circular model* and *modular model.*

Linked teams. Variation of the linear model in which different subgroups, or teams, achieve various subgoals in sequential manner.

Minutes. Report of meeting actions of a substantive nature.

Modular model. Group organizational structure designed to allow multifaceted goals to be divided into various subgoals which are independently achieved. See also *circular model* and *linear model.*

Morale. Emotional state of an individual or group as shown through willingness to work, confidence, manner, etc.

New business. Agenda term used for any item of business not previously considered.

Old business. Agenda term used for any item held over for consideration from a previous meeting.

Ownership. Belief that a problem or task is possessed and controlled by an individual or group.

Pencil-and-paper survey. Any of several types of written questionnaires used to gather information on a variety of topics; distinguished from interviews and other person-to-person information-gathering techniques.

Pie chart. Illustration showing the relationship of informational parts to the whole. Example: A pie chart could be used to show how individual elements of the school budget are spent in relationship to the total budget.

Presentation skills. Knowledge and abilities needed to perform the dual role of leader/spokesman; skills include writing, speaking, management and organization, and public relations know-how.

Principal-centered, principal-directed. School administrator determined content and direction, usually in reference to a staff meeting.

Principal's cabinet. See *advisory board.*

Quality circle. Structured group approach to problem identification and solution, taking its basic organization from similar models in the business sector.

Recommendation (level of authority). Middle level of authority; group conclusions produce suggestions for consideration in an external—i.e., nongroup—decision process. See *levels of authority.*

Segregated file. Method of storing information according to main and subcategories.

Seminar. Meeting, or series of meetings, devoted to study and exchange of ideas on one or more educational topics.

Shared responsibility. Underlying assumption that group work, in order to be successful, depends upon the mingling of diverse talents, needs, and interests; mutually supportive and interactive teamwork.

Spokesperson. One who serves as a contact person or liaison to persons outside the group or individual being represented; serves as reporter to present information to external publics.

Staff meeting. Forum for discussion and resolution of problems and questions arising out of the business of education.

Standing committee. Committee formed for a long-term goal, usually extending for several months or years. See *advisory board*, as an example of a standing committee.

Steering committee. See *advisory board*.

Subcommittee. Smaller group within a larger committee; comparable to a *team* in task force terminology. See *team*.

Superintendent's cabinet. Advisory board formed at the district level. See *advisory board*.

Survey. Any information gathering form utilizing systematic questions and answers. Example: yes–no questionnaires, rankings, checklists, opinionnaires.

Tangibility (of workshop products). Documentable outcomes, not necessarily reducible to "paper" products.

Task force. Group of individuals charged with the responsibility of developing new policies, programs, plans, or procedures in matters relevant to the school.

Team. Subgroup of a task force, usually consisting of two to four individuals working toward a particular subgoal of the total group.

Topical. (1) Focused on a particular topic or subject; (2) "of the moment"; of current interest or importance.

Workshop. Meeting, or series of meetings, devoted to the development of a specific educational product.

Workshop characteristics. (1) Product-oriented; (2) group-oriented; (3) education-oriented.

An Easy Guide to Proper Meeting Procedures

Appendix B

MEETINGS that follow an orderly course are usually more productive than those which are simply allowed to "happen." This orderly course can be directed through two procedures: (1) the agenda or order of business and (2) the rules of order or procedures by which business is conducted.

Figure B-1 lists the components of a standard agenda in the order that they might expect to be considered.

Roll Call
Minutes of Previous Meeting
Financial Report
Standing Committee Reports
Special Committee Reports
Old Business
New Business

FIGURE B-1. Agenda Items and Order

NOTE: Speakers in the assembly address the chair, never the house.

Motion	Interrupt the speaker?	Second needed?	Debatable?	Amendable?	Vote required?
Principal motion	No	Yes	Yes	Yes	Majority
aSuspend further consideration ("table")	No	Yes	No	No	Majority
aEnd debate	No	Yes	No	No	Two-thirds
aPostpone consideration to a certain time	No	Yes	Yes	Yes	Majority
aRefer to a committee	No	Yes	Yes	Yes	Majority
aAmend	No	Yes	Yes	Yes	Majority
aAmend an amendment	No	Yes	Yes	Yes	Majority
bAdjourn	No	Yes	No	No	Majority
bRecess	No	Yes	No	Yes	Majority
bRaise a question of privilege; complain about noise, room temperature etc.	Yes	No	cNo	No	Decision of chair
dObject to procedures	Yes	No	No	No	Decision of chair

FIGURE B-2. Standard Meeting Rules

Motion	Interrupt the speaker?	Second needed?	Debatable?	Amendable?	Vote required?
dRequest information	eYes	No	No	No	No vote
dCall for division, an actual count to verify a voice vote	fNo	No	No	No	Chair decides unless challenged; then 2/3 vote
dObject to consideration	Yes	No	No	No	Two-thirds
dConsider tabled motion	No	Yes	No	No	Majority
dReconsider a motion already voted on	Yes	Yes	Yes, if original motion was debatable	No	Majority
dSuspend rules or reorder agenda	No	Yes	No	No	Two-thirds
dAppeal a ruling of the chair	Yes	Yes	Yes	Yes	Majority

aThese are referred to as subsidiary motions.
bThese are called privileged motions.
cMotions which result are debatable.
dThese are incidental or unclassified motions.
eOnly if urgent; otherwise, no.
fThis motion must be made before the next item of business is taken up.

FIGURE B-2. (continued)

In many instances, certain agenda items may be omitted. Any group's order of business is directed by the nature of the group. Likewise, some elements of the agenda—roll call, for example—will be handled informally. In a small committee meeting, it would be foolish to *call* roll when attendees can be recorded simply by glancing around the table. Similarly, many group meetings dispense with reading the minutes by distributing printed minutes prior to the meeting. The financial report may be handled in like manner.

Particularly in the meetings of small groups, shortcuts can be taken in procedure without doing harm to the procedural intent. A good rule of thumb governs these adaptations: The smaller the meeting, the more informal the procedure; the larger the meeting, the more formal the procedure.

Because *How to Build Staff Involvement in School Management* is concerned primarily with smaller groups, such as committees, task forces, advisory boards, and so on, it is not necessary here to review completely the standard rules of order for business meetings. Instead, Figure B-2 is an attempt to present those procedural guidelines which are most often needed and used by smaller group meetings. A fuller review can be obtained in most libraries from a current edition of *Robert's Rules of Order*, the classic manual of parliamentary procedure written by General Henry M. Robert and originally published in 1907. Numerous revisions and adaptations have been published over the years.

Some groups find it helpful to reproduce and distribute procedural rules, such as those shown in Figure B-2, so that members may be familiar with them. Certainly, the procedures should be fully understood by group leaders, so that smooth, organized progress can be guaranteed.

Here is a checklist for meeting leaders that may be helpful:

_____ Did I prepare an agenda and communicate it to the group?

_____ Did I include all the agenda elements that were needed?

_____ Did I follow the agenda during the meeting?

_____ Did I adhere to the procedural rules established by or for the group?

_____ Did I maintain order by calling on speakers systematically and not allowing extraneous conversations?

_____ Did I attempt to allow equal voice from all sides during debate?

_____ Did I rule fairly and consistently when called upon to do so?

_____ Did I ensure that accurate minutes were taken so that a record of the meeting was maintained?

Leaders who chair meetings will find that *yes* answers to these questions help to ensure that meetings move easily and accomplish their objectives.

Selected Resources

Appendix C

SEVERAL useful books can be found on the market today that will supplement the material contained in *How to Build Staff Involvement in School Management*. Here are ten that seem to be most effective in supporting or extending ideas presented in this text. They are arranged in alphabetical order by title, beginning—coincidentally—with the author's previous book.

Complete Book of School Public Relations: An Administrator's Manual and Guide by Donovan R. Walling. (Englewood Cliffs, New Jersey: Prentice-Hall, Inc., 1982.)

Because public relations includes an organization's internal public (i.e., staff), many of the administrative strategies presented in this book are applicable to building staff involvement in school management as well. In particular, the group techniques used in school public relations will be germane to broader contexts.

Of particular interest is the A.I.M. plan of action for program development, including the organization of a school public relations task force. Planning strategies, using grouping techniques, comprise the first five chapters of *Complete Book of School Public Relations*.

Conceptual Blockbusting by James L. Adams. (New York: W. W. Norton and Company, 1976.)

Subtitled "A Pleasurable Guide to Better Problem Solving," Adams' book is an excellent source of basic information about problem-solving strategies. Many examples and exercises are provided that make the text come alive for the reader.

The author's approach to problem solving is to discuss ways that solutions are blocked. Some chapter titles illustrate this notion: "Perceptual Blocks," "Cultural and Environmental Blocks," "Emotional Blocks," and so on. How these various types of blocks are dealt with is the substance of the book—hence the title, *Conceptual Blockbusting.*

Managerial Psychology by Harold J. Leavitt. Fourth Edition. (Chicago: University of Chicago Press, 1978.)

While there are any number of competent managerial psychology books on the market nowadays, this particular volume appears to be one of the most down-to-earth ones. Where other such books seem distinctly "organization-oriented," Leavitt's book feels much more "people-oriented." This feeling is immediately reinforced by the title of Part 1: "People One at a Time, the Units of Management."

Leavitt touches on many elements related to staff involvement in the management process, including problem solving, authority, and organization. Part 3, entitled "People in Threes to Twenties, Efficiency and Influence in Groups," is an especially useful section.

Quality Circles: A Team Approach to Problem Solving by Frank M. Gryna, Jr. (New York: AMACOM, 1981.)

This monograph is a research study published by a division of American Management Associations. As with the previous work, *Managerial Psychology*, the frame of reference is the world of business and industry, but similarly many features are applicable to school management also. As noted in Chapter Nine of *How to Build Staff Involvement in School Management*, a number of school districts are now implementing variations of the quality circle concept.

Gryna's 96-page treatment of the subject provides an excellent overview of this Japanese business innovation. The monograph is a good starting point for investigating the characteristics and potential of quality circles.

School Administration: Challenge and Opportunity for Leadership by Richard A. Gorton. (Dubuque, Iowa: Wm. C. Brown Company, 1976.)

Basically a textbook on school administration, Gorton's work focuses primarily on principalship. The six major parts of the book run the gamut from "Purpose/Direction/Accountability" to "Career Considerations." As a general resource for school management, the book is excellent.

Staff involvement themes are touched upon in Part 3, "Staff Personnel and Instructional/Curricular Leadership." Noteworthy are "Administrator-Staff Relations" (Chapter 9) and "Supervision of Instruction" (Chapter 11). Excellent, thought-provoking material.

Successful School Communications: A Manual and Guide for Administrators by William Goldstein and Joseph C. DeVita. (West Nyack, New York: Parker Publishing Company, 1977.)

Two school principals, Goldstein and DeVita, discuss a variety of strategies for communication with students, staff, and parents.

Chapters dealing with faculty-administrator interaction and preparing public presentations are especially useful.

Supervision: The Reluctant Profession by Ralph L. Mosher and David E. Purpel. (Boston: Houghton Mifflin Company, 1972.)

Mosher and Purpel's book is an intriguing look at educational supervision and well worth placement on the must-read list for both teachers and administrators.

Chapter Seven is entitled, "Supervising Teachers in Groups." Here, the authors discuss mutual learning, problem solving, and other concepts related to working with staff groups. The entire book, however, is appropriate reading for anyone interested in sound supervisory practices.

T.E.T. (Teacher Effectiveness Training) by Dr. Thomas Gordon. (New York: Peter H. Wyden, 1974.)

Since its publication, Gordon's book has become a classic in the field of education. While the focus is on teachers, the concepts effectively apply to managers in education as well. In terms of staff involvement, Chapter Eleven, "Making the School a Better Place for Teaching," offers many positive approaches to group work.

An earlier book by this same author might also prove interesting and informative; it is called *Group Centered Leadership: A Way of Releasing the Creative Power of Groups.*

Theory Z by William Ouchi. (Reading, Massachusetts: Addison-Wesley Publishing Company, 1981.)

This book has been widely acclaimed in business circles recently as the successor to quality circles. Subtitled "How American Business Can Meet the Japanese Challenge," it is obviously business-oriented, but many of the concepts can be applied to education—just as quality circle techniques are now finding their way into school districts.

In fact, the people-focused nature of education makes schools more likely places for Theory Z practices than most businesses. Ouchi's book is highly readable and full of useful anecdotes taken from the author's personal experiences in observing firsthand many Japanese companies. It may not be strictly educational reading, but it is good reading for educators.

What Every Supervisor Should Know by Lester R. Bittel. (New York: McGraw-Hill Book Company, 1980.)

As is the case with some of the other books mentioned in this resource section, this one is written for supervisory personnel in business and industry. However, it too contains many excellent ideas and techniques that can be applied to working with professional educators. Of particular interest will be the first six chapters, collectively entitled, "Supervisory Management and Human Relations."

Specific chapters of note include: "Individual Motivation," "Work Group Behavior," and "Conflict and Cooperation."

Index

T

U

V